Contents

UNIT 1

Consonants, Hard and Soft c and g

Theme: Celebrations

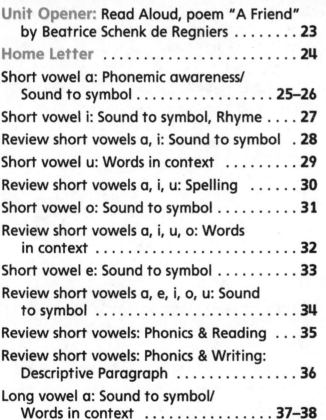

UNIT 2

Short and Long Vowels

Theme: Friends and Family

Compounds, Syllables, Blends and Digraphs, Y as a Consonant and Vowel, R-controlled Vowels

UNIT 3

Theme: What an Imagination!

UNIT 4

Contractions, Plurals, Suffixes

Theme: A Working World

UNIT 5
Vowel Pairs, Digraphs, Diphthongs
Theme: By the Sea!

Prefixes, Base Words, Suffixes, Syllables

Theme: Taking Care of Our Earth

Synonyms, Antonyms, Homonyms, Homographs, Dictionary Skills

Theme: Express Yourself!

Read Aloud

CHINESE NEW YEAR

Colorful dancing lions and dragons weave down the street. There is music and dancing. People wave and cheer. It's Chinese New Year!

People celebrate Chinese New Year for 15 days. It is a time to wish their friends and family good luck.

Part of celebrating Chinese New Year is eating a special meal. People wear the color red to bring happiness. They also decorate their homes with special flowers to bring good luck.

Maybe the best part of Chinese New Year is lucky money. Money is placed into little red packets. A good luck message is written on the front. Then the packets are given to children.

TALK About It

What part of Chinese New Year would you like the best? Why?

Dear Family,

In this unit about "Celebrations," your child will learn about consonants that appear at the beginning, middle, and end of words. Your child will also learn about the hard and soft sounds for the letters **c** and **g** in words such as coat, circus, giraffe, and gate. As your child becomes familiar with identifying consonants, you might try these activities together.

▶ Make a mobile to celebrate your child's favorite day. With your child, draw pictures or cut pictures from magazines. Punch a hole in the pictures and tie them to a coat hanger. Ask your child to name each picture and identify any consonants at the beginning, middle, or end of the name.

▶ Your child might enjoy reading these books with you. Look for them in your local library.

Children Just Like Me: Celebrations!
by Anabel Kindersley

Light the Candle! Bang the Drum! by Ann Morris

Sincerely,

_____

Estimada familia:

En esta unidad, que trata sobre "Celebrations" ("Celebraciones"), su hijo/a estudiará las consonantes que aparecen al principio, mitad y final de las palabras. También aprenderá los sonidos fuertes y débiles de las letras **c** y **g** en palabras como coat (abrigo), circus (circo), giraffe (jirafa) y gate (puerta). A medida que su hijo/a se vaya familiarizando con la identificación de consonantes, pueden hacer las siguientes actividades juntos.

▶ Construyan una escultura con partes movibles para celebrar el día favorito de su hijo/a. Juntos, dibujen o recorten ilustraciones de revistas. Perforen un hueco en la ilustración y unánla a un perchero. Pidan a su hijo/a que nombre cada ilustración e identifique las consonantes al principio, mitad o final del nombre.

▶ Ustedes y su hijo/a disfrutarán leyendo estos libros juntos. Búsquenlos en su biblioteca local.

Children Just Like Me: Celebrations!
de Anabel Kindersley

Light the Candle! Bang the Drum!
de Ann Morris

Sinceramente,

_____

Name _____

> Say the name of each picture. Write the capital and small letter for the beginning sound of each picture.

1.
___ ___

2.
___ ___

3.
___ ___

4.
___ ___

5.
___ ___

6.
___ ___

7.
___ ___

8.
___ ___

9.
___ ___

10.
___ ___

11.
___ ___

12.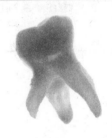
___ ___

13.
___ ___

14.
___ ___

15.
___ ___

16.
___ ___

> **Circle each word that begins with q, s, v, w, y, or z.**

1. The Quinns were excited about their summer vacation.

2. They were going to Washington, D.C., for seven days.

3. Susan wanted to visit the home of the President.

4. Zack couldn't wait to see their cousins Vincent and Sally.

5. Mom said they would all see the Washington Monument.

6. Dad was sure they would like to sail on the river.

7. The whole family wanted to visit the zoo.

8. Zack said the zebra was his very favorite animal.

9. His sister wanted to see a wolf with yellow eyes.

10. Soon it was time for the Quinns to go.

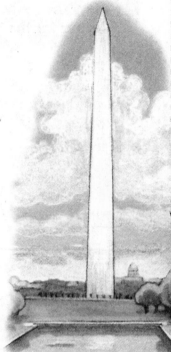

> **Choose two of the sentences above. Write the numbers of the sentences in the left-hand corners of the boxes. Then draw a picture to go with each sentence.**

Initial consonants: Words in context

HOME

Say aloud: *Quinns, summer, visit, wolf, yellow, zoo.* Invite your child to name another word with the same beginning sound as each of these words.

Name_____

> Say the name of each picture. Write the consonant that
> stands for the sound you hear in the middle of each word.

1.
_____

2.
_____

3.
_____

4.
_____

5.
_____

6.
_____

7.
_____

8.
_____

9.
_____

10.
_____

11.
_____

12.
_____

13.
_____

14.
_____

15.
_____

16.
_____

Medial consonants: Sound to symbol   9

Look at the picture. Read the sentence. Circle the word that will finish the sentence. Write it on the line.

1. Mom took my _____ sister and me to the zoo.

baby   bunny

2. The zoo is in the center of our _____.

cousin   city

3. First we saw a _____ at the zoo.

tiger   tulip

4. Then we came to the pond where the _____ lives.

honey   beaver

5. Next we saw a big cat called a _____.
It was covered with spots!

leopard   lemon

6. After that we saw a _____ beside a cactus.

lizard   peanut

7. I got to ride on a _____.

parrot   camel

8. As we left, my sister _____ good-bye
to the animals.

waved   wagon

TALK About It   Do you think the family had fun at the zoo? Why?

HOME   Help your child to use three of the answer words in a sentence.

Name _____

> Look at the letter in each row. Then, say the name of each picture.
> Color the pictures whose names end with the sound of the letter.

1.

t

2.

k

3.

p

4.

x

  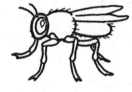 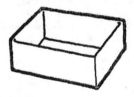

5.

l

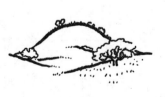   

Look at the picture. Fill in the circle beside the word that will finish the sentence. Write the word on the line.

1. Ben rides the _____ to school.
- ○ bug
- ○ bud
- ○ bus

2. He is wearing his red _____.
- ○ cat
- ○ cap
- ○ car

3. Ben carries his lunch in a _____.
- ○ bat
- ○ bad
- ○ bag

4. Today he has a _____ sandwich.
- ○ ham
- ○ hat
- ○ had

5. Ben writes with his new _____.
- ○ pet
- ○ pen
- ○ peg

6. He labels a _____ with it.
- ○ map
- ○ man
- ○ mat

7. After school, Ben plays with his _____.
- ○ car
- ○ cat
- ○ cap

8. At eight o'clock he goes to _____.
- ○ beg
- ○ bet
- ○ bed

TALK About it **How is your school day like Ben's?**

 HOME Ask your child to think of words ending with the letters *t, k, p, x,* and *l.*

Name _____

Say each word in the box below. Write the words that contain a hard **c** sound under the picture of the cap. Write the words that contain a soft **c** sound under the picture of the cereal.

RULE

When the letter **c** is followed by the vowels **a**, **o**, or **u**, it has a hard sound. Hard **c** has a **k** sound. When **c** is followed by **e**, **i**, or **y**, it usually has a soft sound. Soft **c** has an **s** sound.

cat   cot   cut
lace   city   fancy

actor	cattle	cinema	cub	doctor	pencil
candy	celery	coat	cymbal	grocery	price
carriage	cellar	corn	decide	palace	recess
		cow	decorate		

_____ _____

_____ _____

_____ _____

_____ _____

_____ _____

_____ _____

_____ _____

_____ _____

Hard and soft c: Sound to symbol   **13**

RULE

When the letter **g** is followed by the vowels **a**, **o**, or **u**, it has a hard sound. When **g** is followed by **e**, **i**, or **y**, it usually has a soft sound. Soft **g** has the sound you hear at the beginning of **jam**.

gain　　**g**ot　　**g**um
a**g**e　　**g**iant　　**g**ypsy

▶ **Say the words in each box. Draw a line to connect the words that have the same g sound.**

1.		2.	
page	game	figure	large
flag	engine	gold	giraffe
3.		4.	
orange	gym	gutter	ago
sugar	organ	pigeon	arrange

▶ **Write the words from above in the correct columns.**

Hard g　　　　Soft g

Hard and soft g: Sound to symbol

HOME

Encourage your child to use some of the words on this page in sentences.

Name_____

Circle each word that has the soft c sound or the soft g sound.

When the letter **c** or **g** is followed by **e**, **i**, or **y**, the **c** or **g** usually has a soft sound.
ra**ce**   pa**ge**

ice	can	lace	came	fancy	gym
gate	giant	rice	large	huge	wig
rage	center	celery	because	coyote	general
hug	city	judge	page	face	cookies
game	engine	dance	leg	ceiling	police
fence	garden	stage	guess	magic	place
tag	nice	bridge	giraffe	gem	cover

Circle each word that has the hard sound of c or g.

1. Everyone had a good time at Carol's birthday party.

2. The guests came dressed in fancy costumes.

3. Lance was a detective who solved crimes.

4. Janice wore a colorful gown and an orange wig.

5. A magician did tricks and juggled cans.

6. The children played games and had sack races.

7. Carol's mother gave them cake and ice cream.

8. Carol gasped as she opened her cards and presents.

9. Curtis gave her a goldfish in a bowl.

10. Gary the cat looked at it closely.

11. He thought he could catch the fish for dinner.

12. The children laughed when Gary was carried outside.

Do you think everyone had a good time at the party? Why or why not?

Hard and soft c and g:
Words in context, critical thinking   **15**

Read the clue. Write a word from the box that matches the clue.

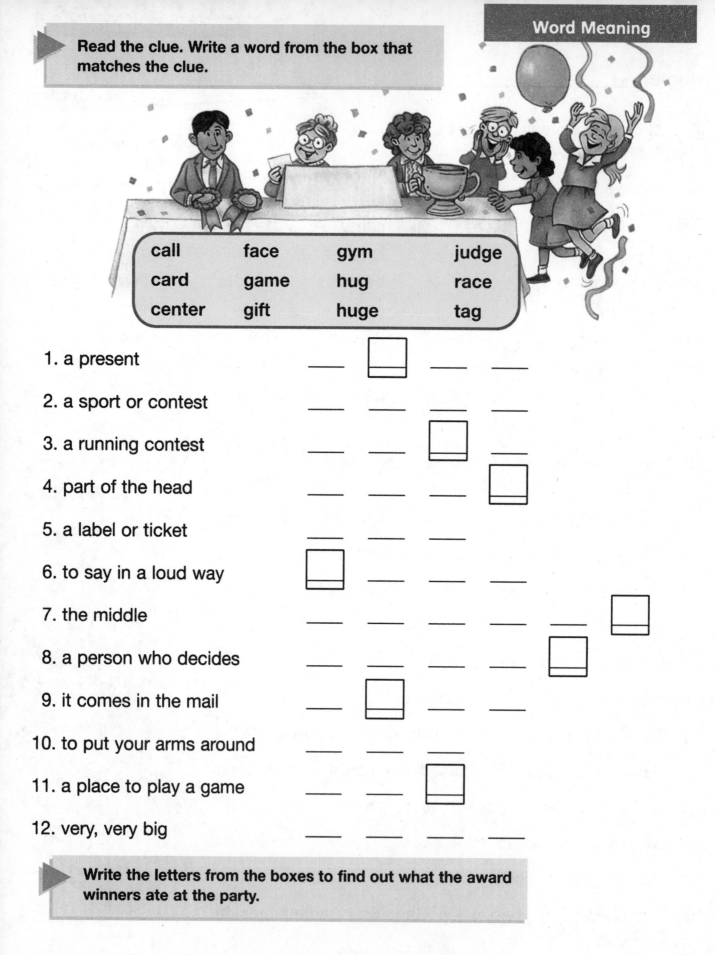

call	face	gym	judge
card	game	hug	race
center	gift	huge	tag

1. a present   _ ☐ _ _

2. a sport or contest   _ _ _ _

3. a running contest   _ _ ☐ _

4. part of the head   _ _ _ ☐

5. a label or ticket   _ _ _

6. to say in a loud way   ☐ _ _ _

7. the middle   _ _ _ _ _ ☐

8. a person who decides   _ _ _ _ ☐

9. it comes in the mail   _ ☐ _ _

10. to put your arms around   _ _ _

11. a place to play a game   _ _ ☐

12. very, very big   _ _ _ _

Write the letters from the boxes to find out what the award winners ate at the party.

_ _ _ _ _ _ _ _ _

Choose words from the word box and ask your child to tell you if the word has a hard or soft sound for c or g.

Name_____

 Phonics & Spelling

Read the words. Write each word under the heading where it belongs.

candy	cement	corn	game
guess	gym	page	price

Soft c   **Soft g**   **Hard g**   **Hard g**

1. _____   2. _____   3. _____   4. _____

5. _____   6. _____   7. _____   8. _____

Read the words. Write each word under the heading where it belongs. You will write some of the words two times.

balloon	cement	dragon	leaf	lizard
ruler	seven	parrot	zipper	radio

Consonant in the Middle

9. _____   10. _____   11. _____

12. _____   13. _____   14. _____

15. _____   16. _____   17. _____

Consonant at the End

18. _____   19. _____   20. _____

21. _____   22. _____   23. _____

24. _____   25. _____   26. _____

Phonics & Writing

A journal is a special book where you can keep any kind of writing—words, lists, drawings, poems, stories, even doodles. A **journal entry** is something you write in a journal.

Write a journal entry about a celebration you have been to. Some of the words in the box may help you.

balloon	games	party	birthday	cake	gym
slice	holiday	candles	magic	family	fun

Start your entry with the date.

Your entry can be **notes, lists,** or **whole sentences**.

Make doodles or drawings if you want to.

Ask your child to read the journal entry he or she wrote.

Name _____

Come Celebrate

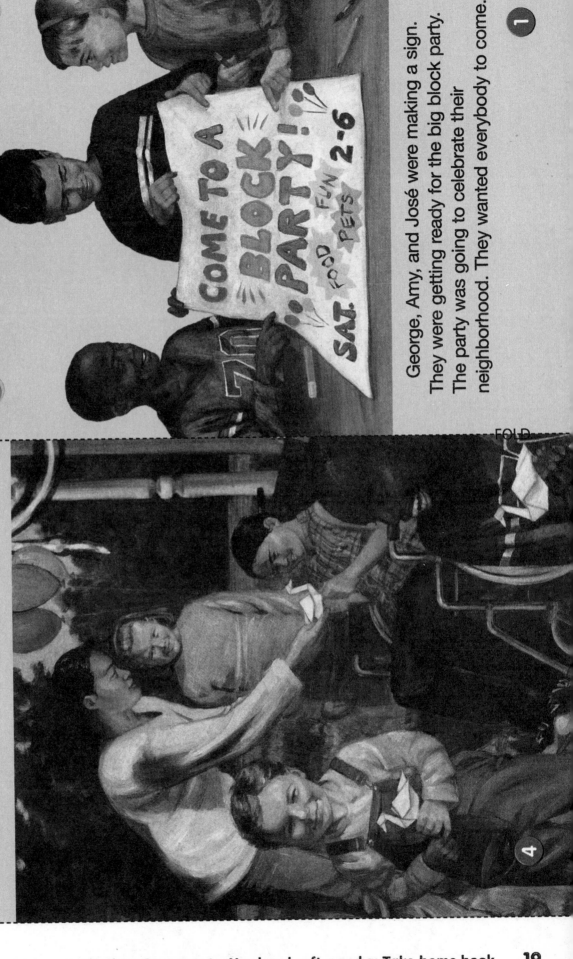

George, Amy, and José were making a sign.
They were getting ready for the big block party.
The party was going to celebrate their
neighborhood. They wanted everybody to come.

1

FOLD

At the end of the day, all the neighbors were
happy and proud. The block party had gone
very well. Then Mrs. Ito had a wonderful
surprise. She gave all the children birds made of
paper to help them remember this day forever.

4

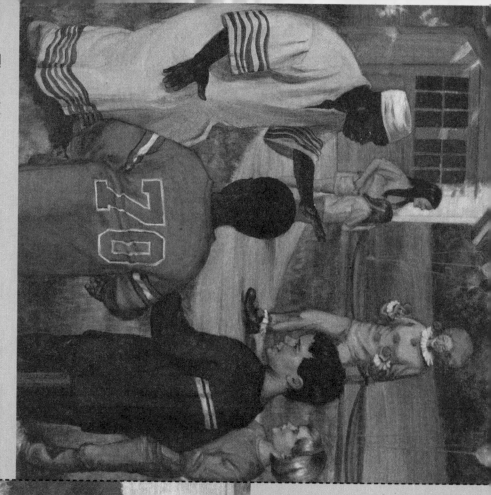

The adults brought the food. There were hotdogs and hamburgers and corn, beans, and rice. Everything tasted so good!

The pet parade was a great hit. There were dogs and cats and a lizard or two. There was a parrot that could talk. There was a soft rabbit. The children paraded through the street with their pets. Everyone waved as they went by.

The children all helped to decorate the street. They hung streamers and balloons that waved in the breeze. Music filled the air. It was almost time for the party.

Everyone came. Mr. Addo told stories. Mrs. Stone juggled colorful balls. There were games and contests, too.

2

3

Name_____

> Read the words in the box and think about whether the consonants are at the beginning, middle, or end of each word. Write the word in the column or columns that show the position of the consonants. You will write some words more than once.

vat	gas	soap	pedal	leaf	hurry
wagon	zoo	cab	yellow	jiffy	dog
hated	funny	happy	room	music	comic
near	cowboy	jazz	tow	bike	hazy

Beginning Consonant	Middle Consonant	Ending Consonant

p
1. _____ 2. _____ 3. _____

d
4. _____ 5. _____ 6. _____

b
7. _____ 8. _____ 9. _____

l
10. _____ 11. _____ 12. _____

m
13. _____ 14. _____ 15. _____

s
16. _____ 17. _____ 18. _____

r
19. _____ 20. _____ 21. _____

n
22. _____ 23. _____ 24. _____

g
25. _____ 26. _____ 27. _____

t
28. _____ 29. _____ 30. _____

z
31. _____ 32. _____ 33. _____

f
34. _____ 35. _____ 36. _____

Initial, medial, and final consonants: Assessment   **21**

 Fill in the circle beside the word that belongs in each sentence.

1. Alice ____ a package for her birthday. ○ got   ○ gym

2. She was ____ that it was from Carl. ○ curtain   ○ certain

3. The package was ____! ○ huge   ○ hug

4. Alice tried to ____ what was in it. ○ gem   ○ guess

5. She ____ opened the enormous box. ○ cement   ○ carefully

6. A ____ orange kite was inside. ○ giant   ○ garden

7. "I ____ believe it," Alice exclaimed. ○ cent   ○ can't

8. "I'll ____ Carl right away to thank him." ○ call   ○ cell

Write all of the word choices listed above in the correct columns.

9. **Hard c**

_____

_____

_____

_____

10. **Soft c**

_____

_____

_____

_____

11. **Hard g**

_____

_____

_____

12. **Soft g**

_____

_____

_____

Read Aloud

A Friend
by Beatrice Schenk de Regniers

Whoever we are,
Whatever we be,
We're friends 'cause I'm me
We're friends 'cause she's she.
(Or because he is he—
Whatever, whatever the case may be.)
A friend
is a friend
is a friend!

TALK About It

What special things do you do with your friends?

Dear Family,

In this unit about "Friends and Family," your child will learn about the vowels **a**, **e**, **i**, **o**, and **u** and the sounds they make. As your child becomes familiar with vowel sounds, you might try these activities together.

▶ Make a collage of activities that your child shares with family or friends. With your child, identify the activities whose names have short vowel sounds. Help him or her to draw pictures or cut pictures from magazines and glue them on paper. Then repeat the activity to illustrate long vowel sounds.

▶ With your child, read the poem on page 23 and identify the words with long and short vowel sounds.

▶ Your child might enjoy reading these books with you. Look for them in your local library.

26 Fairmount Avenue
by Tomie De Paola

Horrible Harry Moves Up to Third Grade
by Suzy Kline

Sincerely,

_____

Estimada familia:

En esta unidad, que trata sobre "Friends and Family" ("Amigos y familia"), su hijo/a estudiará las vocales **a**, **e**, **i**, **o** y **u** y sus sonidos. A medida que su hijo/a se vaya familiarizando con los sonidos de las vocales, pueden hacer las siguientes actividades juntos.

▶ Construyan un collage de las actividades que su hijo/a comparte con la familia y amigos. Juntos, identifiquen las actividades en cuyos nombres hay vocales con sonidos breves. Ayuden a su hijo/a hacer dibujos o recortar ilustraciones de revistas y pegarlas sobre papel. Después, repitan la actividad para ilustrar las vocales con sonidos largos.

▶ Lean con su hijo/a el poema en la página 23 e identifiquen las palabras con sonidos breves y con sonidos largos.

▶ Ustedes y su hijo/a disfrutarán leyendo estos libros juntos. Búsquenlos en su biblioteca local.

26 Fairmount Avenue de Tomie De Paola

Horrible Harry Moves Up to Third Grade de Suzy Kline

Sinceramente,

_____

Name _____

> Say the name of each picture. Color each picture whose name has the short sound of **a**.

1. 	2. 	3. 	4. 
5. 	6. 	7. 	8. 
9. 	10. 	11. 	12. 

> Circle the words with a short **a** in the puzzle. Use the words in the box to help you.

```
B   A   T   C   F
H   R   Q   A   A
A   X   R   T   N
N   H   A   T   W
D   C   A   K   E
G   L   A   S   S
```

ax	glass
bat	hand
cat	hat
fan	cake

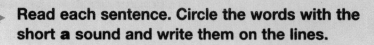

Read each sentence. Circle the words with the short a sound and write them on the lines.

Sound to Symbol

1. Ann had fun at the beach on Sunday.

_____ _____ _____

_____

2. She ran with her friends Vicky and Jack.

_____ _____ _____

_____

3. Dad helped them make sand castles.

_____ _____ _____

_____

4. Then the children swam fast to the raft.

_____ _____ _____

_____

5. They napped in the van on the ride back home.

_____ _____ _____

What else can you do at the beach?

Have your child select two or three of the short *a* words and think of some words that rhyme with them.

26   Short vowel a: Sound to symbol, critical thinking

Name_____

> Write the name of each picture. Then, circle the vowel in each word you wrote.

1.

_____

2.

_____

3.

_____

4.

_____

5.

6.

7.

8.

> Say each word in the first column. Find a word in the second column that rhymes with it. Draw a line to connect the two words.

9.		10.		11.		
kick	fig	hip	tin	wig	hit
rip	hill	pin	big	lit	rig
dig	sick	pig	sip	dip	bin
bill	lip	did	lid	tin	tip

Short vowel i: Sound to symbol, rhyme   **27**

Say the words in the box below. Write the words with a short **a** sound under the picture of the cat. Write the words with a short **i** sound under the picture of the fish.

lamp	late	Jim	gift	if	back
bike	cake	cat	ham	died	zip
hit	map	rain	an	sip	tick
ask	dime	fish	milk	ran	at
pin	dish	wax	will	rap	flat

Short **a**

Short **i**

_____ _____ | _____ _____

_____ _____ | _____ _____

_____ _____ | _____ _____

_____ _____ | _____ _____

_____ _____ | _____ _____

HOME Ask your child to think of some names for the cat and the fish using short *a* and short *i* words.

Name _____

▶ Write the name of each picture. Then, circle the vowel in each word you wrote.

1.	2.	3.	4.
_____	_____	_____	_____

5.	6.	7.	8.
_____	_____	_____	_____

▶ Fill in the circle beside the word that belongs in each sentence. Write the word on the line.

9. _____ is a very large duck.

○ Gas
○ Gus
○ Got

10. He likes to sleep in the _____.

○ sick
○ sun
○ sad

11. One day he tried to swim in a _____.

○ tan
○ tub
○ tent

12. It was too small, so he got _____.

○ stick
○ stuck
○ stack

13. What bad _____ for a very large duck!

○ luck
○ lick
○ lock

Say each word. Change the short **u** to short **a**. Write the new word in the first column. Then, change the short **a** to short **i**. Write the new word in the second column.

	Short **a** word	Short **i** word
1. fun	fan	fin
2. us		
3. bug		
4. hum		
5. hut		
6. but		
7. luck		
8. tuck		
9. bun		
10. lump		
11. bud		
12. rug		
13. must		
14. stuck		
15. truck		
16. pun		

Pick a few groups of words and help your child think of rhymes for each word such as *fun/bun, fan/pan, fin/pin*.

Name_____

▶ Write the name of each picture. Then, circle the vowel in each word you wrote.

1.  _____	2. _____	3.  _____	4. _____
5.  _____	6.  _____	7.  _____	8.  _____

▶ Read the paragraph. Underline the words with the short **o** sound. Then write the words on the lines.

A Summer Picnic

The Todd family went on a picnic one summer day. Although the sun was shining brightly, it was not too hot. They ate a big lunch with hamburgers, juice, and salad. After lunch, Dot and Tim helped Mom search for unusual rocks. They stored these in a big box. Dad and Bobby went to the pond with their dog to watch the ducks. They saw a toad hop in the grass. It was a great day!

9. _____   10. _____   11. _____

12. _____   13. _____   14. _____

15. _____   16. _____   17. _____

18. _____   19. _____   20. _____

Make two new words by changing the vowel in each word to a, i, u, or o.

1. cat _____ _____

2. bad _____ _____

3. tip _____ _____

4. lock _____ _____

5. on _____ _____

6. big _____ _____

7. ham _____ _____

8. fun _____ _____

 Find the word in the box that will finish each sentence. Write the word on the line.

9. I love my tabby _____, Max.

10. He sleeps _____ the rug in my room.

11. Sometimes Max plays with a paper _____.

12. He likes to _____ in and out of it.

13. I gave _____ some string to play with, too.

14. It was _____ to see Max try to catch it.

15. Once Max was very _____.

16. He jumped on _____ of the counter.

17. He made some milk _____ over.

18. I was going to _____ the floor.

19. Then Max started to _____ up the milk.

20. He cleaned the mess _____ a hurry!

bad	bag	cat
fun	him	in
lick	mop	on
run	tip	top

 Do you think Max is a good pet? Why or why not?

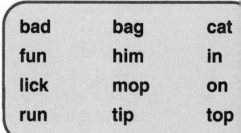 Ask your child to write a story using some of the words from the box.

Name_____

> Write the name of each picture. Then, circle the vowel in each word you wrote.

1.

_____

2.

_____

3.

_____

4.

_____

5.

_____

6.

_____

7.

_____

8.

_____

> Say each picture name. Write two words from the box that rhyme with the name.

fed	den	red
pet	pen	let

9. _____

10. _____

11. _____

12. _____

13. _____

14. _____

Read the words in the box. Write the words with the same short vowel sound in the correct list. Then, write your own word with the same vowel sound on the last line.

top	fit	bus	cab	cup
jet	pen	pig	rock	wig
tub	box	tag	step	map
bed	him	nut	pot	sad

short a

short e

short i

_____

_____

_____

_____

_____

_____

_____

_____

_____

_____

_____

_____

short o

short u

_____

_____

_____

_____

_____

_____

 Ask your child to list the words in the box in alphabetical order.

Name _____

 **Phonics & Reading**

Read the story. Use words with short vowels to finish the sentences.

Living in the Trees

Squirrels, birds, and monkeys can all make their homes in trees. Did you know that some people build homes in trees, too? Of course, people do not build nests as birds do! They build tree houses.

Some people live in their tree houses all the time. Others build tree houses to have a place just to relax. Many parents build tree houses so their children can have a fun place to play. There are even tree houses that can be rented for a very different kind of vacation!

Whether a tree house is just for fun or a place to live, it must be built with care. It is important to pick only the strongest branches of a tree to hold up the tree house. The branches must not move around too much in the wind, or the house will move too!

1. People do not build _____ as birds do.

2. Some people _____ in their tree houses all the time.

3. Other people build tree houses to have a place _____ to relax.

4. Many parents build tree houses so their children _____ have a fun place to play.

5. The branches that hold up the tree house must _____ move around in the wind.

 What do you think it would be like to live in a tree house?

Review short vowels: Reading, critical thinking

A **descriptive paragraph** uses words to create a picture for the reader. The words tell how something feels, looks, sounds, smells, and tastes. One sentence gives the topic. The other sentences give details about the topic.

▶ Write a descriptive paragraph about a trip you would like to take with friends or family. Some of the words in the box may help you.

trip	sun	picnic	pond
city	swam	tent	fun
bus	napped	hot	fish

Begin with a **topic sentence** that tells what you are describing.

Give **details** about the topic in the other sentences.

Use some **describing words** to make a clear picture of your topic.

_____

_____

_____

_____

_____

_____

_____

_____

_____

_____

HOME Ask your child to read the descriptive paragraph to you and point out the words with short vowel sounds.

Name _____

Circle the word that names each picture.

1.
pail
paid
pal
paste

2.
ran
rain
rake
rail

3.
stay
stamp
strain
spray

4.
trade
trail
traffic
tray

5.
sail
say
sad
safe

6.
cape
cane
case
can

7.
plant
plate
plane
pain

8.
race
raft
rain
rare

9.
tape
tap
plate
pat

10.
ray
train
ran
take

11.
tail
tan
tame
tape

12.
hail
day
had
hay

Read each sentence. Underline the words with the long a sound. Then, write them on the lines below the sentence.

1. Kate could hardly wait until the first of May.

_____   _____   _____
_____

2. She and Gail would see their first baseball game.

_____   _____   _____
_____

3. The Braves would play the Jays.

_____   _____   _____
_____

4. When the day finally came, it looked like rain.

_____   _____   _____
_____

5. Just in case, the girls decided to take their gray caps.

_____   _____   _____
_____

6. They arrived late and paid at the gate.

_____   _____   _____
_____

7. They raced to claim their places.

_____   _____   _____
_____

8. A batter named Dave got on first base.

_____   _____   _____
_____

9. He waved when he made it to home plate.

_____   _____   _____
_____

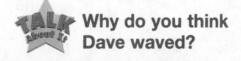 **Why do you think Dave waved?**

 Ask your child to use other long *a* words, or words from the page, to continue the story.

Name _____

> **Circle the word that names each picture.**

1.
kit

kite

2.
ride

rid

3.
pine

pin

4.
rip

ripe

5.
bit

bite

6.
fir

fire

7.
Tim

time

8.
pile

pit

9.
dime

dim

10.
sit

site

11.
fine

fin

12.
slide

slid

Long and short vowel i: Sound to symbol

Find the word in the box that will finish each sentence. Write the word on the line.

1. Kay got a new _____ to fly.

2. It came in the _____ from Mike.

3. A big smile was on Kay's _____.

4. The kite had a long _____.

5. It had blue and red _____.

6. It also had _____ yellow stars.

7. Kay had to _____ a string to it.

8. She flew it on a very windy _____.

9. The wind stopped, and the kite _____ down.

10. Then it began to _____, and Kay ran home.

11. She carefully put the kite _____.

12. Kay _____ at the thought of flying it again.

away
came
day
face
five
kite
mail
rain
smiled
stripes
tail
tie

Circle each word that has a long vowel sound.

13. whale   pie   pail   big   pig   fine

14. jam   blame   nine   bike   dime   gas

15. hit   save   fist   pipe   trip   man

16. sand   mice   plate   fish   cat   trash

17. ate   name   dish   five   game   snap

18. ran   hand   map   rain   pain   line

HOME

With your child, take turns saying as many words as you can that have the long *a* sound.

Name _____

Look at the picture. Circle the word that names the picture. Then, complete the sentence by writing the word on the line.

RULE

If a one-syllable word has two vowels, the first vowel usually stands for the long sound, and the second vowel is silent. If the first vowel is **u,** the word has the long **u** sound. Long **u** can have the sound of **oo,** as in **blue,** or **yoo,** as in **cute.**

tube   glue   fruit

1.

luck

Luke

_____ will play a song at his concert.

2.

sun

Sue

He will play the song with

_____ .

3.

flute

flunk

They will play the _____ .

4.

sit

suit

Luke will wear his new _____ .

5.

cut

cute

He will also get his hair _____ for the concert.

6.

hug

huge

After the concert, his dad will give him

a big _____ .

7.

fun

fruit

Then Luke will have _____ juice and cookies.

 How do you think Luke will feel after the concert?

Say each word in the box and listen for the long vowel sound. Then, write the word in the correct column.

cane	tune	dime	stay	ride	mule	fine
bike	lake	pail	use	tape	lie	came
tube	pie	suit	tuba	like	cube	rain

Long a

Long i

Long u

1. _cane_

8. _bike_

15. _tube_

2. _____

9. _____

16. _____

3. _____

10. _____

17. _____

4. _____

11. _____

18. _____

5. _____

12. _____

19. _____

6. _____

13. _____

20. _____

7. _____

14. _____

21. _____

Say each word. Write two words that rhyme with it.

lake

like

suit

22. _____

24. _____

26. _____

23. _____

25. _____

27. _____

Ask your child to add more rhyming words to the lists above.

Name _____

▶ **Circle the name of each picture.**

> **RULE**
> If a one-syllable word has two vowels, the first vowel usually stands for the long sound, and the second vowel is silent. If the first vowel is **o**, the word has the long **o** sound.
>
> b**o**n**e**   g**oa**t   t**oe**

1.
   ripe
   rap
   rope
   rode

2.
   row
   ray
   rod
   rule

3.
   soap
   soak
   sap
   sip

4.
   bow
   bone
   bun
   box

5.
   hive
   hop
   hay
   hose

6.
   robe
   rope
   rob
   rod

7.
   bone
   bat
   boat
   bite

8.
   tone
   toe
   toad
   tie

9.
   cane
   cone
   can
   came

10.
    doe
    den
    dock
    duck

11.
    corn
    cook
    coat
    cube

12.
    got
    goal
    game
    gas

Say each word. Find the word in the box that rhymes with it. Then, write the rhyming word on the line.

1.

cone	coat	row
rode	hope	pole

load _____

boat _____

hoe _____

bone _____

soap _____

hole _____

2.

pail	late	made
lake	way	save

wait _____

day _____

sale _____

cake _____

paid _____

wave _____

3.

like	hive	ride
mine	bite	pie

dive _____

lie _____

line _____

bike _____

tied _____

kite _____

4.

tune	tube	mule
rude	cute	use

June _____

rule _____

mute _____

cube _____

fuse _____

dude _____

Review long vowels a, i, u, o

HOME

Help your child use rhyming words from the page to make up sentences such as *I like the bike.*

Name _____

> Look at the picture. Circle the word that names the picture. Then, complete the sentence by writing the word on the line.

1.

Pet
Pete

_____ likes to visit the zoo.

2.

seals
sells

He thinks the _____ are funny.

3.

set
seat

Pete finds a _____ to watch them play.

4.

tent
teeth

He likes the lion with its big _____.

5.

meat
met

The lion likes to eat _____.

6.

eagle
enter

Pete's favorite animal is the _____.

7.

trend
tree

It sits high up in a _____.

8.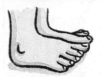

fell
feet

Pete's _____ hurt at the end of the day.

 What is your favorite animal at the zoo? Why?

Say the name of each picture. Color the animals whose names contain the long vowel sound shown at the beginning of each row.

1.

Long a

jay   snail   cat   whale

2.

Long i

tiger   mice   kitten   pig

3.

Long u

skunk   mule   duck   puppy

4.

Long o

fox   goat   doe   ox

5.

Long e

seal   hen   bee   eagle

46   Review long vowels a, e, i, o, u

 Invite your child to use each of the words with a long vowel sound in a sentence.

Name _____

Phonics & Spelling

Find a word from the box to complete each clue. Write the words in the puzzles.

| bell | day | hand | luck | ride | boat | flute | kick |
| pile | tape | team | cone | gift | lock | pond | tent |

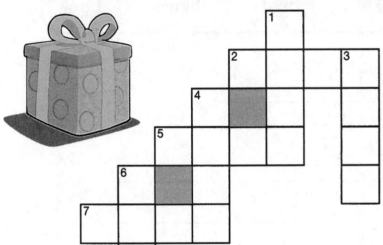

Across
2. ring the ___
5. wrap a ___
7. ___ the door
8. wave your ___

Down
1. sleep in a ___
3. good ___
4. ___ the ball
6. fish ___

Across
2. ice-cream ___
4. cut the ___
6. a sunny ___
7. play the ___

Down
1. row the ___
3. ___ the bus
5. put papers in a ___
8. ___ players

Review short and long vowels: Spelling   **47**

Making **lists** can help you learn. They can help you organize your thoughts and remember important facts and ideas. Items on a list are often numbered.

Make a list of some things you like to do at home. Some of the words in the box may help you.

read	help	cook	play	ball	cat
dog	home	like	best	things	book

Begin by writing the **topic** of your list.

_____

Begin each item on a new line.

Number the items on your list.

HOME

Ask your child to read the list and identify the words with long and short vowels.

Animal Homes

Animals live in many different kinds of homes. Some animals build their homes, while others live in trees or under the ground.

Some animals that build their own homes are beavers and spiders. Beavers build their homes from sticks and mud. Many spiders spin webs and live in or near the webs.

1

Some animals have two homes that are very far apart. Monarch butterflies and Arctic terns are two kinds of animals that travel a long way to a warmer winter home.

Every year, some monarchs make a trip of 3,000 miles to their winter homes in Mexico. The Arctic terns travel even farther. Each winter they fly from their homes near the North Pole to warmer homes near the South Pole. Their trip is over 10,000 miles long each way!

4

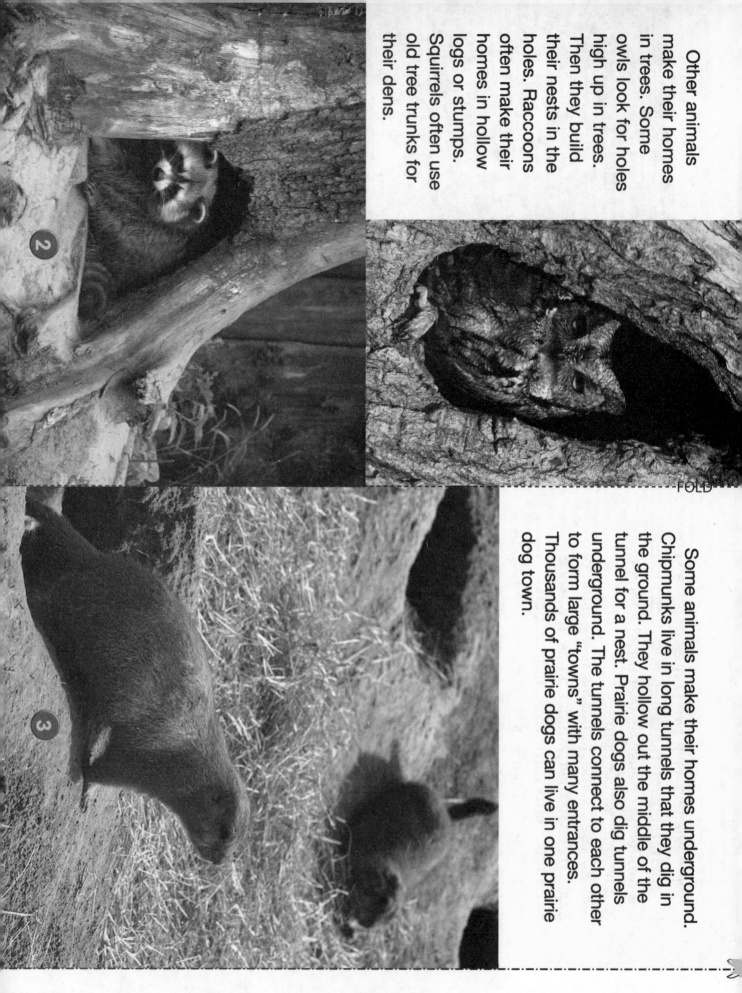

Other animals make their homes in trees. Some owls look for holes high up in trees. Then they build their nests in the holes. Raccoons often make their homes in hollow logs or stumps. Squirrels often use old tree trunks for their dens.

FOLD

Some animals make their homes underground. Chipmunks live in long tunnels that they dig in the ground. They hollow out the middle of the tunnel for a nest. Prairie dogs also dig tunnels underground. The tunnels connect to each other to form large "towns" with many entrances. Thousands of prairie dogs can live in one prairie dog town.

2

3

Name_____

Say the name of each picture. Circle the word that tells if the vowel sound is short or long. Then, write the picture name on the line.

1.

short   long
_____

2.

short   long
_____

3.

short   long
_____

4.

short   long
_____

5.

short   long
_____

6.

short   long
_____

7.
short   long
_____

8.

short   long
_____

Say each word. Add a letter to change it to a word with a long vowel sound. Write the new word on the line.

9. cap _____

10. ran _____

11. tap _____

12. tub _____

13. cub _____

14. hug _____

15. got _____

16. hop _____

17. fed _____

18. hid _____

19. set _____

20. kit _____

21. can _____

22. bit _____

23. met _____

 Say the first word in each row. Fill in the circle beside the word with the same vowel sound.

1.	**can**	○ mail	○ gas	○ name	○ tape
2.	**rust**	○ suit	○ mule	○ hum	○ use
3.	**deep**	○ peak	○ went	○ sled	○ elf
4.	**milk**	○ pipe	○ hike	○ file	○ hill
5.	**cute**	○ nuts	○ fuse	○ shut	○ dull
6.	**clock**	○ cone	○ goat	○ dot	○ soak
7.	**desk**	○ peel	○ neck	○ leap	○ tree
8.	**last**	○ cake	○ rain	○ bank	○ same
9.	**fire**	○ hid	○ ship	○ fill	○ kite
10.	**job**	○ plot	○ note	○ soap	○ rode
11.	**mug**	○ glue	○ cube	○ flute	○ luck
12.	**flake**	○ black	○ race	○ ask	○ fan
13.	**will**	○ mist	○ shine	○ white	○ dime
14.	**send**	○ seen	○ meat	○ bet	○ jeep
15.	**joke**	○ box	○ spot	○ rock	○ coat

UNIT 3

Compounds, Syllables,
Blends and Digraphs, Y as
a Consonant and Vowel,
R-controlled Vowels
Theme: What an Imagination!

Read Aloud

The Spangled Pandemonium

by Palmer Brown

The Spangled Pandemonium
Is missing from the zoo.
He bent the bars the barest bit,
And slithered glibly through.

He crawled across the moated wall,
He climbed the mango tree,
And when his keeper scrambled up,
He nipped him in the knee.

To all of you a warning
Not to wander after dark,
Or if you must, make very sure
You stay out of the park.

For the Spangled Pandemonium
Is missing from the zoo,
And since he nipped his keeper,
He would just as soon nip you.

TALK About It

Would you see a Spangled
Pandemonium at the zoo?
Why or why not?

Dear Family,

In this unit about "Imagination," your child will learn about compound words such as sunshine and basketball; syllables in words such as pen/cil; **y** as a consonant and as a vowel as in carr**y** and wh**y**; consonant blends and digraphs as in **bl**anket and e**ch**o; and **r**-controlled vowels as in g**ar**den and b**ir**d. As your child becomes familiar with these concepts, you might try these activities together.

▶ Help your child make a collage showing pictures of words that have **r**-controlled vowels such as star, tiger, turkey, garden, park, soccer.

▶ Help your child identify some of the words in the poem on page 53 that begin with two consonants and make a list of the consonant pairs.

▶ Your child might enjoy reading these books with you. Look for them in your local library.

Meanwhile, Back at the Ranch by Trinka Hakes Noble

The Mysterious Tadpole by Steven Kellogg

Sincerely,

Estimada familia:

En esta unidad, que trata sobre "Imagination" ("Imaginación"), su hijo/a estudiará palabras compuestas como sunshine (rayos del sol) y basketball (baloncesto); sílabas en palabras como pen/cil (lápiz); **y** como una consonante y como una vocal como en carr**y** (llevar) y wh**y** (por qué); combinaciones y digramas de consonantes como en **bl**anket (manta) y e**ch**o (eco); y combinaciones de vocales y **r** como en g**ar**den (jardín) y b**ir**d (pájaro). A medida que su hijo/a se vaya familiarizando con estos conceptos, pueden hacer las siguientes actividades juntos.

▶ Construyan con su hijo/a un collage que muestre dibujos de palabras con combinaciones de vocales y **r** como star (estrella), tiger (tigre), turkey (pavo), garden (jardín), park (parque), soccer (fútbol).

▶ Ayuden a su hijo/a a identificar algunas de las palabras que comienzan con dos consonantes en el poema de la página 53 y hagan una lista de las parejas de consonantes.

▶ Ustedes y su hijo/a disfrutarán leyendo estos libros juntos. Búsquenlos en su biblioteca local.

Meanwhile, Back at the Ranch de Trinka Hakes Noble

The Mysterious Tadpole de Steven Kellogg

Sinceramente,

Name _____

Say each compound word. On the lines, write the two words that make up the compound word. Then, circle the words with short vowel sounds. Underline the words with long vowel sounds.

A **compound word** is made up of two or more words joined together to make a new word. **Homework** is **work** you do at **home**.

1. teapot _____ _____

2. sunshine _____ _____

3. seagull _____ _____

4. beehive _____ _____

5. beanbag _____ _____

6. pancake _____ _____

7. wayside _____ _____

8. airway _____ _____

9. necktie _____ _____

10. milkweed _____ _____

11. peanuts _____ _____

12. treetop _____ _____

13. waterfall _____ _____

14. overcoat _____ _____

Compound words   **55**

> **Read each clue. Match each compound word from the box to its clue. Write the word on the line.**

backpack	backyard	bathtub	countertop	dustpan
outside	overhead	paintbrush	raincoat	rattlesnake
seashell	snowflake	shoelace	treetop	waterfall

1. a brush for painting _____

2. the top of a tree _____

3. opposite of inside _____

4. a coat worn in rain _____

5. a pan to scoop dust _____

6. a shell near the sea _____

7. a flake of snow _____

8. a tub for a bath _____

9. a snake with a rattle _____

10. the top of the counter _____

11. a pack on your back _____

12. the back of the yard _____

13. over your head _____

14. water that falls _____

15. a lace for a shoe _____

HOME Make up clues your child can answer with compound words, such as *a boat that sails. (sailboat)*

Name _____

Say the name of each picture. Write the number of syllables you hear in the box.

1.

□

2.

□

3.

□

4.

□

5.

□

6.

□

7.

□

8.

□

9.

□

10.

□

11.

□

12.

□

13.

□

14.

□

15.

□

16.

□

Look at each word. Write the number of vowels you **see** in the first column. Say the word. Write the number of vowels you **hear** in the second column. Then, write the number of syllables in the third column.

	Vowels You See	Vowels You Hear	Number of Syllables
1. basket			
2. jeep			
3. milk			
4. rabbit			
5. basement			
6. music			
7. beans			
8. hillside			
9. mailbox			
10. peanuts			
11. picnic			
12. ate			
13. pancake			
14. sailboat			
15. tune			
16. rode			
17. treetop			
18. cabin			

 Ask your child to tell you a story using six words on this page.

Name _____

> Write the name of each picture. Circle the **r** blend that stands for the beginning sound.

1.
_____

3.
_____

5.
_____

2.
_____

4.
_____

6.
_____

> Find the word or words in the box that will complete each sentence. Write the words on the lines.

| brother | crowds | dream | friends | from |
| practice | prize | proud | trumpet | try |

7. My _____ Tim and I play in the school band.

8. We both play the _____.

9. We will _____ hard for the big parade.

10. There will be a _____ for the best band.

11. We _____ of winning it.

12. _____ of people will watch _____ the sidewalks.

13. All our _____ will cheer for us.

14. We will _____ hard to make them _____ of us.

Read each clue. Find a word in the box that matches the clue. Write the word on the line. Circle the **r** blend that stands for the beginning sound.

| frame | crow | broom | bridge | grapes |
| train | truck | drum | grasshopper | bride |

1. You can cross over me.

I am a _____.

2. I ride on the road.

I am a _____.

3. I hold a picture.

I am a _____.

4. I am a big black bird.

I am a _____.

5. We are fruits on the vine.

We are _____.

6. You sweep the floor with me.

I am a _____.

7. I ride on tracks.

I am a _____.

8. It is my wedding day.

I am a _____.

9. I am a green bug.

I am a _____.

10. You play me with sticks.

I am a _____.

 Ask your child to name other words that begin with the *r* blends *br, cr, dr, fr, gr,* and *tr.*

Name_____

Write the name of each picture. Circle the
l blend that stands for the beginning
sound in its name.

Remember that in a **consonant blend**
the sounds of the consonants blend
together, but you can still hear each
sound. Listen for the l blends in the
following words.

black   **pl**ant

1.

_____

2.

_____

3.

_____

4.

_____

5.

_____

6.

_____

7.

_____

8.

_____

9.

_____

10.

_____

11.

_____

12.

_____

13.

_____

14.

_____

15.

_____

For each word, find two words in the clock with the same l blend. Write them on the lines.

block   glow
flag   blue
sleep   play
clean   please
slide   glue
fly   clip

1. clock   _____   _____

2. black   _____   _____

3. flat   _____   _____

4. glad   _____   _____

5. plant   _____   _____

6. sled   _____   _____

 Read each sentence carefully. Find the word in the glass that will complete the sentence. Write the word on the line.

7. The wind was _____ as Flora left school.

8. The sky was covered with stormy _____ .

9. It was too cold to _____ outside.

10. Flora _____ her hands into her pockets.

11. She had left her _____ at home.

12. Flora's house was six _____ away.

13. She was _____ when she finally arrived.

14. Her mom gave her a _____ of warm milk.

15. Flora sat _____ to the fireplace to get warm.

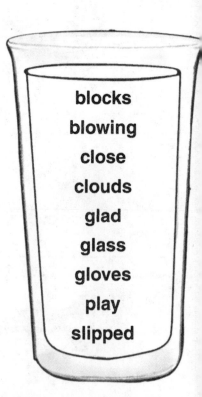

blocks
blowing
close
clouds
glad
glass
gloves
play
slipped

 Ask your child to add one new word to each group of words at the top of the page.

Name_____

Write the name of each picture. Circle the **s** blend that stands for the beginning sound.

1.
_____

2.
_____

3.
_____

4.
_____

5.
_____

6.
_____

7.
_____

8.
_____

9.
_____

10.
_____

11.
_____

12.
_____

13.
_____

14.
_____

15.
_____

Read each sentence. Circle the word that will complete the sentence. Write the word on the line.

1. Our first camping trip was (special, slender). _____

2. We (stamp, spent) five days in the mountains. _____

3. Our trip was in early (string, spring). _____

4. The weather was (still, spill) quite chilly. _____

5. We wore (scatters, sweaters) under our coats. _____

6. We also wore two pairs of (stockings, snails). _____

7. I tripped on a (stump, sport) while hiking. _____

8. My ankle became very (swollen, squirrel). _____

9. We all (swept, screamed) when we saw a snake. _____

10. The snake just (splashed, slithered) away. _____

Read each word. Circle the s blend that is used in the word. Write the word on the line.

11. skid _____   12. stamp _____

13. smile _____   14. spray _____

15. scale _____   16. stream _____

17. sniff _____   18. spell _____

19. sweep _____   20. scrub _____

21. smell _____   22. snow _____

HOME Help your child use s-blend words from the page to make up silly sentences, such as *The slender squirrel smiled.*

Name _____

Write the name of each picture. Circle the consonant blend that stands for the ending sound.

1.
_____

2.
_____

3.
_____

4.
_____

5.
_____

6.
_____

7.
_____

8.
_____

9.
_____

10.
_____

11.
_____

12.
_____

13.
_____

14.
_____

15.
_____

16.
_____

Final consonant blends   **65**

Read the poem. Underline the words with the **fl** consonant blend. Then write the words on the lines. Use each word only once.

A fly and a flea flew up in a flue.
Said the fly to the flea, "What shall we do?"
"Let's fly," said the flea.
"Let's flee," said the fly.
So they fluttered and flew up the flue.

1. _____   2. _____   3. _____

4. _____   5. _____   6. _____

 Write your own nonsense poem. Choose words from the box or your own words with beginning or ending consonant blends. Write the words on the lines.

chimp	chomp	jump	stamp	stomp	cling
skunk	snail	snake	stew	sled	spoon
grabbed	grapes	grew	gruff	sped	spider
spin	spoke	twiggy	twirled	twisted	sloth

7. A _____ and a _____ _____ in a _____.

8. Said the _____ to the _____, "What shall we do?"

9. "Let's _____," said the _____ to the _____.

10. "Let's _____," said the _____ to the _____.

11. So they _____ and _____ up the _____.

Ask your child to read his or her poem to you, stressing the words with consonant blends.

Name_____

▶ **Add y to each blend to make a word.
Write the word on the line.**

> **RULE**
>
> When **y** is the only vowel at the end of a syllable or a word of one syllable, **y** has the long **i** sound.
>
> tr**y**ing   sh**y**

1. fr _____

2. cr _____

3. tr _____

4. dr _____

5. sk _____

6. sl _____

7. fl _____

8. spr _____

▶ **Read each question. Use one or more of the words you just made to answer it. Write your answer on the lines. Use a complete sentence.**

9. Where do you look to see clouds?

_____

_____

10. Why do we use umbrellas when it rains?

_____

_____

11. What can an airplane do in the sky?

_____

_____

12. What sometimes happens if you fall and hurt yourself?

_____

_____

Say each word in the box and listen for the **y** sound. Write the words in the correct column.

bunny	cry
every	grocery
trying	muddy
shy	sky
swiftly	why

Y = Long i

_____

_____

_____

_____

_____

Y = Long e

_____

_____

_____

_____

_____

Find a word in the box below to complete each sentence. Write the word on the line.

1. My _____ likes to do things together.

2. Sometimes we go to the _____.

3. There are so _____ books to choose from.

4. Dad likes _____ books about ancient Egypt.

5. I like books with lots of _____ jokes.

6. Mom likes books about _____ gardens.

7. Once we checked out more than _____ books.

8. It was difficult to _____ them!

| carry |
| family |
| funny |
| history |
| library |
| many |
| pretty |
| twenty |

HOME Ask your child to use some words that end in *y* to describe an activity that your family likes to do together.

Y as a vowel: Long i and e, Words in context

Name _____

Say the name of each picture. Find the name in the box. Write it on the line. Circle the names that have **y** as a consonant.

When **y** comes at the beginning of a word, it is a consonant.

yolk

yo-yo	bunny	yarn	cry	fly	yes
penny	pony	pretty	yard	sky	try

1.

_____

2.

_____

3.

_____

4.

_____

5.

_____

6.

_____

7.

_____

8.

_____

Say the first word in each row. Circle the words that have the same **y** sound.

9.	**yes**	sky	yard	yellow	windy
10.	**many**	pretty	yet	dry	sweetly
11.	**fly**	lovely	yell	try	why
12.	**happy**	sorry	every	yard	fry
13.	**year**	many	yolk	funny	yarn

Read the story. Underline each word that has a y. Then, write the words in the correct columns.

Goody's Ice Cream

One afternoon my brother and I saw a plane go over our yard.
"Isn't it a beauty, Craig?" I yelled over the noise.
"Where is it now?" I heard Craig cry out.
"Over there, in the sky above the yellow house," I said. "Do you see it yet?"
"I would like to fly a plane like that one," said Craig.
"Let's try to save so we can have our own plane when we grow up. Here's twenty cents to start," I said.
Just then, from down the street came the jingling of a bell and the sound of a whistle. We both knew that it was Goody, the person who sold ice cream. The ice-cream bars were big and thick and creamy. Craig looked at me. "Why not?" I said. "It is very hot and dry."
We stood eating our ice cream. Craig said, "We'd better start soon to save for the airplane, or we'll be fifty years old before we get it."
"Yes," I said. "We'd better start early tomorrow."

Y = a consonant	Y = long e	Y = long i

Review y as a vowel and as a consonant

Make up a story with your child using some of the words in the columns.

Name_____

> **Write the name of each picture. Then circle the digraph.**

1.

2.

3.

4.

5.

6.

7.

8.

> **Say each word. Then circle the consonant digraph.**

9. scheme

10. wheel

11. kitchen

12. write

13. birthday

14. threw

15. nickel

16. peaches

17. north

18. finish

19. mother

20. rough

21. beneath

22. choke

23. knit

24. echo

25. know

26. chord

27. thick

28. farther

29. telephone

30. shake

31. wrist

32. chocolate

33. bother

34. ticket

35. wheat

36. chorus

37. tough

38. sign

39. school

40. gnaw

Read each riddle and circle the word to complete the riddle. Write the word on the line, then circle the consonant digraph.

1. What happens when a bowl of fruit is embarrassed?

   The _____ turn red!   cherries   teeth   bananas

2. Why are fish so smart?

   They travel in a _____.   group   school   scheme

3. What's the best thing to put into a pie?

   Your _____!   teeth   knife   fork

4. What bird lowers its head the fastest?

   A _____!   swan   sheep   duck

5. What did the barber say after the near accident?

   "That was a close _____!"   shave   shower   one

6. What always talks back to you?

   An _____!   actor   chorus   echo

7. How do you know owls are curious?

   They're always asking _____.   who   whine   how

8. Why is the sun bright?

   It _____!   bright   shines   shows

Find and circle the words in the puzzle. Use the words in the box to help you.

chorus	nickel
elephant	scheme
gnaw	shower
knife	teeth
laugh	whine

```
E  L  E  P  H  A  N  T
T  A  Z  V  W  L  M  E
N  U  S  C  H  E  M  E
I  G  L  L  I  F  Y  T
C  H  B  G  N  A  W  H
K  N  I  F  E  G  X  L
E  Q  C  H  O  R  U  S
L  S  H  O  W  E  R  Z
```

Ask your child to identify the consonant digraphs in the words in the word box.

Name _____

> Choose a word from the box to complete each sentence.
> Write the word on the line.

1. I love my new elementary _____.

2. My classroom _____ is very nice.

3. Her name is Ms. _____.

4. She _____ how to make learning fun.

5. I like doing _____ problems.

6. In October I was sick with a bad _____.

7. My _____ made me stay in bed.

8. My teacher _____ me a letter.

9. Everyone in my class _____ it.

10. Someone drew a picture of an _____ on it.

11. The picture made me _____.

12. I _____ it was very funny.

cough
elephant
knows
laugh
math
mother
school
signed
teacher
thought
White
wrote

> Say each word. Write its consonant digraph on the line.

13. rough _____

14. kitchen _____

15. Ralph _____

16. choice _____

17. wrong _____

18. tough _____

19. know _____

20. chemical _____

21. sign _____

22. gnaw _____

23. knife _____

24. patch _____

25. phone

26. wrist _____

27. Kathy

Say each word and circle its consonant digraph. Write the word in the column that tells whether the consonant digraph is at the beginning, middle, or end of the word.

beach	another	birthday	starfish	catch
chin	choose	chorus	cough	dishes
elephant	know	laughed	matches	mother
north	path	peaches	rather	tough
shell	sign	threw	together	wheel
whine	white	wish	with	write

Beginning

Middle

End

_____ _____ _____

_____ _____ _____

_____ _____ _____

_____ _____ _____

_____ _____ _____

_____ _____ _____

_____ _____ _____

_____ _____ _____

_____ _____ _____

74   Consonant digraphs: Sound to symbol

HOME
Have your child make up questions that include two or more words from the box, such as *Is a starfish on the beach?*

Name _____

Say the name of each picture. In the first box under the name, write the number of vowels you see in the word. In the second box, write the number of vowel sounds you hear. In the third box, write the number of syllables. The first one is done for you.

1.
telephone

4	3	3

2.
wheat

3.
sandwich

4.
spider

5.
chicks

6.
elephant

7.
fish

8.
umbrella

9.
slippers

10.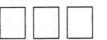
truck

11.
cheese

12.
propeller

13.
knife

14.
blanket

15.
wheel

16.
stove

Circle the two-syllable word that makes sense in the sentence. Write the word on the line.

1. Friday was _____ birthday.

Mother's   my   problem

2. I baked a _____ cake.

chicken   fudge   cherry

3. The cake had _____ candles.

thirty   six   forest

4. Mom loved her _____.

presents   gifts   little

5. I _____ her a picture.

painted   drew   player

6. Dad gave her a blue _____.

kitchen   dress   sweater

7. Grandmother _____ her a red scarf.

never   bought   knitted

 Read the poem. Then, complete each sentence by writing the correct word from the poem on the line.

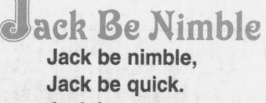

Jack be nimble,
Jack be quick.
Jack jump over
The candlestick.

8. A one-syllable word that means *fast* is _____.

9. The two-syllable word in the title of the poem is _____.

10. The three-syllable word in the poem is _____.

11. A two-syllable word that means *above* or *across* is _____.

HOME

Ask your child to read sentences 1–7 and identify all of the two-syllable words.

Name _____

Read the story. Then, use words with consonant blends or digraphs to finish the sentences.

What an Imagination!

My friend Tony likes to make people laugh. He invents funny stories and jokes to tell. Everyone knows that he has quite an imagination!

One day at recess, Tony said, "You won't believe what happened yesterday when I was walking home from school. Suddenly, I saw a bird with brightly colored feathers. It looked at me and said, 'Hi, Tony! Hi, Tony!' When I blinked, it was gone."

We all laughed and said, "What an imagination you have!"

When we were back in class, Mrs. Kelly asked, "Did anyone see the newspaper story about the parrot that escaped from a pet store yesterday? Luckily, someone recognized the bird and told the owner where to find it. The parrot had the same name as you, Tony."

"See, it wasn't my imagination!" Tony told us. "I just got one fact wrong. The bird wasn't talking to me. It was talking to itself!"

1. Tony likes to make people _____.

2. He invents funny _____ and jokes to tell.

3. Everyone _____ that Tony has quite an imagination.

4. Tony saw a bird on his way home from _____.

5. The bird had brightly colored _____.

6. When Tony _____, the bird was gone.

7. The class told Tony, "_____ an imagination you have!"

8. Tony said he just got one fact _____.

 Why didn't Tony's friends believe his story right away?

Review consonant blends and digraphs: Reading, critical thinking   **77**

Phonics & Writing

A **research report** gives facts and details about a topic. When you write a research report, you find and collect information about a topic that interests you. The information may come from people, books, magazines, newspapers, or the Internet

Write one paragraph for a research report about tigers. The paragraph might be about where tigers live, how they get their food, or something else that interests you about tigers. Some of the words in the box may help you.

white	know	stripes	claws	gnaw
tropics	hunt	travel	protect	must

Give your report a **title**.

_____

Include the **main idea** in your first sentence.

Include **details** about the main idea in the other sentences.

_____
_____
_____
_____
_____
_____
_____
_____

HOME
Ask your child to read the report he or she wrote and identify the words with consonant blends and digraphs.

Name _____

► **Say the name of each picture. Circle the ar, or, ir, ur, or er in each name.**

1.  h o r n	2.  f e a t h e r	3.  b i r d
4.  t i g e r	5.  s t a r	6. n u r s e
7.  b a r n	8.  c i r c u s	9.  t u r k e y

► **Circle each word that contains ar, or, ir, ur, or er. Write the words you circled on the lines.**

10. The storm was over.   _____ _____

11. Sam hurried into the garden. _____ _____

12. He was worried about his turtle. _____ _____

13. The thunder might have scared it. _____ _____

14. Sam carefully looked for it.   _____ _____

15. It was sleeping under a flower. _____

Read each puzzle clue. Find a word in the box that matches the clue. Write the word in the puzzle.

| birds | circus | favorite | garden | park | soccer |
| thirty | tiger | turn | turtle | warm | weather |

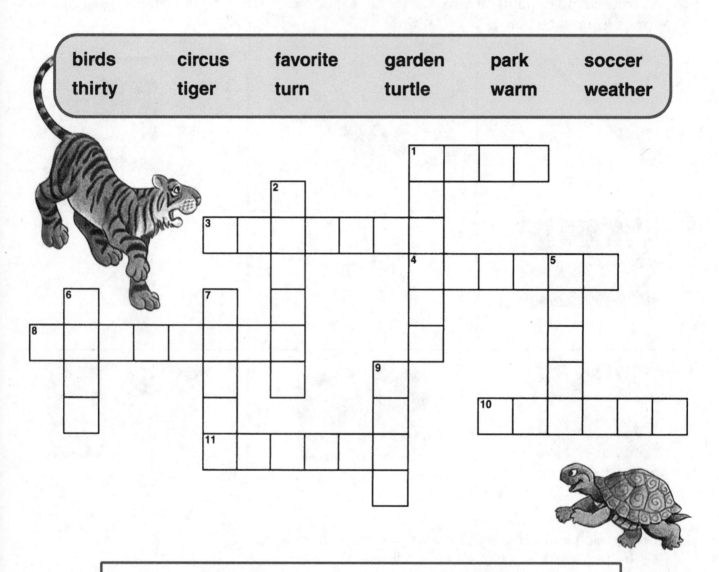

Across

1. move right or left
3. cloudy, windy, or sunny
4. 30
8. most well liked
10. where clowns are found
11. game to kick the ball into the goal

Down

1. an animal with a hard shell
2. plants and flowers
5. a striped wild animal
6. not cool, not hot
7. blue jays and robins
9. a place to play

Ask your child to divide the puzzle words into groups of words with *ar, er, ir, or,* and *ur.*

Name_____

Circle the **ar, or, ir, ur,** or **er** in each numbered word. Then, find the word in the box with the same beginning letter and vowel sound. Write it on the line.

bark	bore	Burt	cord	dart	first	circus
hurdle	leader	herd	purse	shore	startle	thirty

1. f i r _____

2. b u r n _____

3. l e t t e r _____

4. c o r n _____

5. h u r t _____

6. c i r c l e _____

7. d a r k _____

8. s t a r _____

9. b o r n _____

10. s h o r t _____

11. t h i r d _____

12. h e r _____

13. b a r n _____

14. p u r p l e _____

Find a word on the ribbon to complete each sentence. Write the word on the line.

15. My _____ has a green thumb.

16. She loves to work in her _____.

17. Our backyard is beautiful during the _____.

18. It is _____ with colorful flowers!

19. There are _____, yellow, and pink flowers.

20. Mom once won _____ place at a flower show.

21. Her eyes _____ as she received her prize.

bursting

garden

mother

orange

sparkled

summer

third

Read the sentences. Underline each word that contains ar, or, ir, ur, or er. Then write the words you underlined in the correct boxes below.

1. Rita made a special birthday card for a friend.

2. First, she decorated it with blue and red stars.

3. Then, she wrote a clever little verse.

4. In the morning, Rita hurried to the mailbox.

5. Darla received many surprises on Friday.

6. Mom and Dad gave her a purse, a furry kitten, and a red sweater.

7. She got a yellow bird from Aunt Shirley.

8. Darla really likes the large and colorful greeting from Rita.

ir

er

or

ar

ur

R-controlled vowels: ar, er, ir, or, ur,
Sound to symbol

HOME Ask your child to think of one more word to add to each gift box.

Name_____

Say the name of each picture. In the box, write the number of syllables you hear in the picture name. Then, color the pictures whose names have two syllables.

1.

fork ▢

2.

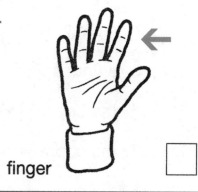

turkey ▢

3.

finger ▢

4.

computer ▢

5.

toaster ▢

6.

letter ▢

7.

star ▢

8.

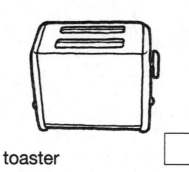

garden ▢

9.

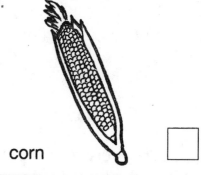

corn ▢

10.

turtle ▢

11.

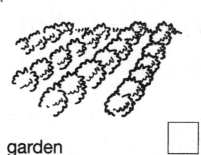

wheelbarrow ▢

12.

circus ▢

R-controlled vowels: Syllables, Sound to symbol

Write the word that matches the meaning. Then say the word. Write the number of syllables in the box.

1. wind, rain, and lightning _____ ☐

2. the day a person is born _____ ☐

3. the day before today _____ ☐

4. red and blue mixed _____ ☐

5. a floor covering _____ ☐

6. the day after Friday _____ ☐

7. the opposite of *tall* _____ ☐

8. the number after 12 _____ ☐

9. musical instrument with strings _____ ☐

10. to surprise and frighten _____ ☐

11. a person who grows crops _____ ☐

12. an animal with a bushy tail _____ ☐

13. corn that is popped _____ ☐

14. a plant with feathery leaves _____ ☐

15. a thing liked the best _____ ☐

16. a place where things are made _____ ☐

17. very shiny _____ ☐

18. a meal eaten at night _____ ☐

19. the opposite of *boy* _____ ☐

20. ships dock here _____ ☐

21. a celebration _____ ☐

birthday
carpet
factory
farmer
favorite
fern
girl
guitar
party
popcorn
port
purple
Saturday
short
sparkling
squirrel
startle
supper
thirteen
thunderstorm
yesterday

Ask your child to identify the *r*-controlled vowel in each word in the box.

Name _____

Phonics & Spelling

Find and circle the hidden pictures. Then write each picture name on the lines below in alphabetical order.

backpack	crow	glove	report	thirty
blanket	dragon	monkey	spoon	tiger
computer	flag	purse	swing	wheel

1. _____   2. _____   3. _____

4. _____   5. _____   6. _____

7. _____   8. _____   9. _____

10. _____   11. _____   12. _____

13. _____   14. _____   15. _____

A **narrative paragraph** tells a story about something that really happened. The events, characters, and setting are real. Often the writer is the main character. Using descriptive words helps bring the story alive.

Write a narrative paragraph about one of the funniest things that ever happened to you. Some of the words in the box may help you.

laughter	favorite	purple	turn	later	yesterday
party	garden	short	dark	first	for

Start your paragraph with a **topic sentence** that tells who, when, and where.

Use words like **first, then,** and **later** to make the order of the story clear.

Use words that tell how things **looked, sounded, smelled, tasted,** and **felt.**

Review r-controlled vowels: Writing

HOME Ask your child to read his or her story to you and identify the words with *r*-controlled vowels.

They Had an Idea!

Did you ever stop to think about how some everyday things came to be? Somebody had to invent, or think up, nearly everything we use.

Think of the plain paper bag. Until the 1860's, paper bags were long and narrow, and people glued them together by hand. Then a woman named Margaret Knight invented a machine that could make paper bags with square bottoms. She made a lot of money. Think about that the next time you use a paper bag!

FOLD

Kathryn "K-K" Gregory became an inventor at the age of 10. One winter day, K-K was playing in the snow. She was upset because the snow kept going up the sleeves of her coat. Then she had an idea. With her mother's help, K-K sewed some cloth sleeves to fit over her hands and forearms. The design was an instant hit! K-K even started her own company to make and sell her invention.

Can you think of a useful solution for an everyday problem? You could be an inventor, too!

...boy, Latimer's favorite activities were drawing and reading. Latimer became a skilled artist who drew plans for inventors. One of the people he worked for was A. G. Bell, inventor of the telephone.

Latimer went on to make his own discoveries. One of his inventions greatly improved the lightbulb. Thomas Edison had already invented a lightbulb, but it was lit by a thin thread of paper that burned out quickly. Lewis Latimer invented a thread made of carbon, which helped the bulb last longer. Thanks to Latimer, electric lights became more popular.

FOLD

Not all inventors are grown-up. Austin Meggitt was only nine years old when he came up with his invention. Austin liked to play baseball, but he had trouble carrying his bat, glove, and ball on his bicycle. He decided he should invent a carrier for his bike that would hold his baseball gear. He named it the "Glove and Battie Caddie." Austin won a prize for his invention. He was also voted into the Inventors Hall of Fame.

Name _____

 Fill in the circle next to the word with a consonant blend that best completes each sentence.

1. Glenn built a wooden _____.
   ○ coat ○ raft ○ left

2. He used _____ to tie it together.
   ○ coat hangers ○ felt ○ string

3. He hoped it would _____.
   ○ float ○ four ○ flee

4. Then the first warm day of _____ arrived.
   ○ winter ○ spring ○ yesterday

5. Glenn carefully pushed his raft into the_____ .
   ○ post ○ pink ○ pond

6. Would it _____ under the water?
   ○ drink ○ sink ○ think

7. Glenn was very happy because it _____ afloat!
   ○ played ○ trapped ○ stayed

8. Glenn is very _____ of the raft he built himself.
   ○ proud ○ sad ○ unhappy

Say each word. Circle the consonant digraph.

9. elephant	10. cheese	11. school	12. knee	13. echo
14. thrush	15. sign	16. tough	17. wren	18. check
19. these	20. whisper	21. match	22. ticket	23. birthday

Consonant blends and digraphs: Assessment   **89**

 Look at the words in the box. Write each word in the correct column.

> beauty   every   fry   spry   year   yesterday

Y = a consonant	Y = long e	Y = long i

1. _____   2. _____   3. _____

4. _____   5. _____   6. _____

Say the first word in each row. Circle the word with the same r sound.

7.	**farm**	parking	worst	third	burn
8.	**corn**	purse	cough	fire	forty
9.	**tiger**	clerk	alarm	snore	park
10.	**squirrel**	wrote	morning	birthday	like

Read the paragraph. Circle the compound words. Write the words on the lines.

Last weekend, my family and I went to the zoo. The day was bright with sunshine, so we didn't need our overcoats. My sister wanted to see the monkeys. The zookeeper told us to look for them in the treetops. All we could see were peanut shells falling from the trees. When we looked up, there were the monkeys!

11. _____   12. _____   13. _____

14. _____   15. _____   16. _____

90   R-controlled vowels, compounds, y as a vowel: Assessment

The Dinosaur Hunters

Imagine that you've just discovered the complete skeleton of a brand-new dinosaur. You'd be famous!

Scientists who study ancient life are called paleontologists (pay-lee-on-TAH-luh-gists). They study fossils, traces of living things that are sometimes found in rocks. Much of their time is spent working in labs or museums. When these scientists do go on a dinosaur "dig," they might spend hours carefully chipping one piece of bone from a rock. Finding a complete skeleton is remarkable.

Still, you might get lucky. That happened to fossil collector Susan Hendrickson. She discovered the finest skeleton of a giant T. Rex ever found. It was nicknamed "Sue" in her honor.

Do you think you would like to become a dinosaur hunter? Why or why not?

Dear Family,

In this unit about "A Working World," your child will learn about contractions, plurals, and suffixes. As your child becomes familiar with these skills and concepts, you might try these activities together.

▶ With your child, draw pictures or cut pictures from magazines to illustrate different kinds of careers. Glue them on sheets of paper, one career per sheet. Then help your child label each page. Staple the sheets together or tie them together with yarn.

▶ Ask your child to read the article on page 91 to you. Help him or her to identify words with contractions and plurals and words with **ed** and **ing.**

▶ Your child might enjoy reading these books with you. Look for them in your local library.

Library Lil by Suzanne Williams

Breakout at the Bug Lab by Ruth Horowitz

Sincerely,

_____

Estimada familia:

En esta unidad, que trata sobre "A Working World" ("Un mundo trabajador"), su hijo/a estudiará contracciones, plurales y sufijos. A medida que su hijo/a se vaya familiarizando con estas destrezas y conceptos, pueden hacer las siguientes actividades juntos.

▶ Con su hijo/a, hagan dibujos o recorten fotos que ilustren diferentes tipos de profesiones. Péguenlos sobre hojas de papel. Después, ayuden a su hijo/a a escribir un título para cada ilustración. Engrapen juntas las hojas o átenlas con un cordón de estambre.

▶ Pidan a su hijo/a que les lea el artículo en la página 91. Ayúdenlo/a a identificar palabras con contracciones, palabras en plural y palabras que terminan en **ed** y **ing.**

▶ Ustedes y su hijo/a disfrutarán leyendo estos libros juntos. Búsquenlos en su biblioteca local.

Library Lil de Suzanne Williams

Breakout at the Bug Lab de Ruth Horowitz

Sinceramente,

_____

Name_____

DEFINITION

Read each contraction. Write the two words that make each contraction. Then write the letter or letters that were left out.

A **contraction** is a short way of writing two words. It is formed by putting two words together and leaving out one or more letters. Use an apostrophe (') to show where something is left out.
I am = I'm   we will = we'll

Contraction	Two Words	Letters Left Out
1. isn't	_____	_____
2. there's	_____	_____
3. haven't	_____	_____
4. wouldn't	_____	_____
5. you've	_____	_____
6. it's	_____	_____
7. let's	_____	_____
8. don't	_____	_____
9. they've	_____	_____
10. couldn't	_____	_____
11. he's	_____	_____

Find a contraction in the word box to match each pair of words. Write the contraction on the line.

1.

isn't	_____ I am
I'm	_____ is not
I've	_____ we are
we're	_____ I have

2.

it's	_____ were not
wouldn't	_____ would not
weren't	_____ it is
didn't	_____ did not

3.

let's	_____ you will
wasn't	_____ you are
we'll	_____ let us
you'll	_____ was not
you're	_____ we will

4.

shouldn't	_____ that is
aren't	_____ they will
that's	_____ will not
they'll	_____ are not
won't	_____ should not

Complete each sentence using a contraction from the box below.

| we'll It's aren't won't I've |

5. _____ going to be a fine day for a hike.

6. _____ been looking forward to it.

7. First _____ walk through the forest.

8. I hope the trails _____ muddy.

9. We _____ get home until evening.

HOME

Ask your child which words make up the contractions in the word boxes.

Name _____

Read the story and circle each contraction. On the lines at the bottom of the page, write the two words that make up each contraction you circled.

A Puzzling Situation

"There's *T. rex!*" said Sam excitedly as he and Alice ran up the stairs in the museum.

"How do scientists put these bones together?" asked Alice.

"It's like a puzzle," said a man behind them. "I'm Dr. West, museum paleontologist. I'd be happy to help you."

"Let's see *Triceratops!*" exclaimed Alice as they walked to the next skeleton.

"Here's an interesting dinosaur," said Sam. "How did you know where each bone would fit?"

"That's a good question," said Dr. West. "It isn't easy, but we're able to use computers to help us with the bones we've found. Then we're ready to solve the puzzle!"

"Wouldn't that be fun to try!" said Alice.

"You're both welcome to watch us someday," said Dr. West. "You'd really enjoy it."

"I think I'll be a paleontologist. Then I'd be a puzzle solver!" said Sam.

"We'll both be puzzle solvers," said Alice quickly. "I'd like to be a paleontologist, too!"

1. _____ 2. _____ 3. _____

4. _____ 5. _____ 6. _____

7. _____ 8. _____ 9. _____

10. _____ 11. _____ 12. _____

13. _____ 14. _____ 15. _____

16. _____ 17. _____ 18. _____

TALK About It Why is a scientist a puzzle solver?

Contractions: 't, 's, 've, 'm, 're, 'll, 'd, critical thinking   **95**

Write the contraction that can be made from the two words.

1. I am _____

2. are not _____

3. can not _____

4. should not _____

5. could not _____

6. did not _____

7. he is _____

8. we will _____

9. does not _____

10. let us _____

11. here is _____

12. you will _____

13. I have _____

14. will not _____

15. you are _____

16. they have _____

17. she is _____

18. we have _____

19. I will _____

20. it is _____

Write a story using five of the contractions that you wrote above.

_____

_____

_____

_____

_____

_____

_____

_____

Ask your child to read the story he or she wrote, and name the words that make up each contraction.

Name_____

Circle the word that names each picture. Then color the pictures that show more than one.

When **s** or **es** is added to a word it forms the plural. Plural means "more than one." See how the ending **s** or **es** makes these words mean more than one.

one pear   two pear**s**
one box   many box**es**

1.

box   boxes

2.

brick   bricks

3.

coat   coats

4.

dish   dishes

5.

letter   letters

6.

grape   grapes

7.

puppet   puppets

8.

egg   eggs

9.

star   stars

10.

gift   gifts

11.

pin   pins

12.

watch   watches

▶ **Write the plural form of the word in parentheses.**

1. five (cross) _____

2. some (glass) _____

3. those (box) _____

4. cake (mix) _____

5. seven (dress) _____

6. few (church) _____

7. three (ax) _____

8. many (dish) _____

▶ **Underline the word in each sentence that means more than one. Then write its base word on the line.**

9. Kim is busy packing boxes. _____

10. She is using bunches of paper. _____

11. She carefully wraps the good dishes. _____

12. She puts paper around the glasses. _____

13. Then she packs her dresses. _____

14. Her favorite is the one with patches on it. _____

15. She does not pack her paintbrushes. _____

16. She ties them together in batches. _____

17. She needs them for her art classes. _____

18. She studies during her lunches. _____

Plurals: Words ending in ss, x, ch, and sh, Words in context

HOME Ask your child to think of more words with plural forms ending in -es.

Name _____

▶ **Write the plural form of the word in parentheses.**

RULE

If a word ends in a consonant and **y**, change the **y** to **i** and add **es**. If a word ends in a vowel and **y**, just add **s**.

one baby   two bab**ies**
one jay   many jay**s**

1. three (cherry) _____
2. some (lily) _____
3. eight (fairy) _____
4. those (fly) _____
5. two (party) _____
6. nine (tray) _____
7. few (boy) _____
8. many (chimney) _____
9. four (day) _____
10. all (turkey) _____

▶ **Underline the word with a suffix in each sentence that means more than one. Then write its base word on the line.**

11. Lucy and Mom went downtown to buy groceries. _____

12. They always had fun on shopping days. _____

13. Lucy saw some puppies in a pet store window. _____

14. Two ladies worked in the store. _____

15. One woman said Lucy could pet the puppies. _____

16. "They're as soft as bunnies," Lucy said. _____

17. Just then two boys came into the store. _____

18. Their families came in, too. _____

19. They had traveled from one of the nearby cities to buy a puppy. _____

Look at each picture. Then read the word below the line. Change the word to mean more than one. Write the new word on the line.

Animals

_____
(puppy)

_____
(turkey)

_____
(bunny)

_____
(monkey)

_____
(jay)

_____
(pony)

Flowers

_____
(daisy)

_____
(lily)

_____
(pansy)

People

_____
(baby)

_____
(boy)

_____
(lady)

Name_____

► **Write the plural form of the word in parentheses on the line.**

1. these (leaf) _____

2. six (calf) _____

3. those (wolf) _____

4. few (knife) _____

5. four (shelf) _____

6. several (elf) _____

7. two (half) _____

8. few (wife) _____

9. ten (thief) _____

10. many (life) _____

► **Write a word from the box below to complete each sentence. Then write its base word on the line.**

calves	knives	leaves
lives	loaves	scarves
shelves	wives	wolves

11. Long ago, pioneers led hard _____.   _____

12. The men built _____ to store things on.   _____

13. They built barns for the cows and their _____.   _____

14. They had to protect the animals from _____.   _____

15. Pioneer _____ worked as hard as their husbands.   _____

16. Each week they baked _____ of bread.   _____

17. They used _____ to cut the bread into thick slices.   _____

18. They made medicine from _____ and roots.   _____

19. At night, the women knitted warm _____.   _____

Read each clue. Find the word in the box that matches the clue. Then, write the word in the crossword puzzle.

elf	thieves	scarves	foxes	loaves
wife	scarf	turkeys	lives	wolf
shelves	axes	elves	car	

Across

1. singular form of elves
4. plural form of thief
7. plural form of scarf
9. singular form of wives
12. plural form of fox
13. plural form of turkey

Down

2. plural form of life
3. plural form of shelf
5. plural form of elf
6. plural form of loaf
8. singular form of scarves
9. singular form of wolves
10. plural form of ax
11. singular form of cars

Ask your child to give the singular and plural forms for names of objects around the home.

Name _____

▶ **Read each word. Make new words by adding the ending s, ed, and ing. Write the new words in the correct columns.**

	s	ed	ing
1. cook	_____	_____	_____
2. jump	_____	_____	_____
3. pick	_____	_____	_____
4. clean	_____	_____	_____
5. help	_____	_____	_____
6. learn	_____	_____	_____
7. play	_____	_____	_____

▶ **Write the base word for each of the following words.**

8. eggs _____		9. hats _____
10. lifts _____		11. makes _____
12. washed _____		13. dreamed _____
14. worked _____		15. burns _____
16. spelling _____		17. stacked _____
18. started _____		19. looking _____
20. dressed _____		21. opening _____
22. runs _____		23. reading _____

DEFINITION

A **suffix** is a word part that is added to the end of a base word to make a new word.

The suffix **er** may be used to compare two things. The suffix **est** may be used to compare more than two things.

▶ Read each sentence. Add **er** or **est** to each word below the line. Write the new word on the line.

1. Lisa is _____ than her sister Nancy.
   (tall)

2. Nancy is _____ than Lisa.
   (old)

3. Their little sister Joy is

   the _____ of the three.
   (young)

4. Joy is also the _____.
   (short)

5. "Lisa may be tall," says Joy, "but I'm

   _____ than she is!"
   (smart)

Lisa   Joy   Nancy

RULE

The suffix **er** sometimes means a *person who*. A teacher is a person who teaches.

▶ Add the suffix **er** to each word. Write the new word on the line.

6. teach _____

7. perform _____

8. sing _____

9. play _____

10. work _____

11. report _____

12. farm _____

13. print _____

HOME Ask your child to make sentences that use the words on the lines above.

Name_____

Circle each word that ends in a single consonant. Then add the suffixes or ending to make new words.

RULE

When a word with a short vowel ends in a single consonant, the consonant is usually doubled before adding a suffix or ending that begins with a vowel.

pet   pet**ted**   pet**ting**

thin   thin**ner**   thin**nest**

ed   **ing**

1. tag _____ _____

2. rip _____ _____

3. jump _____ _____

4. nap _____ _____

er   **est**

5. big _____ _____

6. fat _____ _____

7. cold _____ _____

8. hot _____ _____

Circle the word with a suffix or ending in each sentence. Write its base word on the line.

9. Today was the hottest day of the summer. _____

10. My dog slept longer than he did yesterday. _____

11. A frog skipped by and woke him up. _____

12. He let out a bark and sent it hopping. _____

Complete each sentence by adding the correct suffix or ending to the word in parentheses. Write the word on the line.

1. Ed was tired of _____ on the bench. (sit)

2. He _____ the coach to let him play. (beg)

3. "I'm _____ you in the game," said the coach. (put)

4. On his first try, Ed just _____ the ball. (tip)

5. Then he _____ the ball past the pitcher. (bat)

6. He began _____ and reached home plate. (run)

7. "Ed's our _____player!" said the coach. (hot)

8. Ed was proud to be a _____. (win)

	RUNS	HITS	ERRORS	1	2	3	4	5	6	7	8	9
Home	8	10	4	1	0	1	1	2	1	2		
Visitor	5	9	3	1	2	0	1	0	1			

Write the base word for each of the following words.

9. shopper _____

10. swimmer _____

11. tagged _____

12. stopper _____

13. fanned _____

14. petted _____

15. dripping _____

16. rubbed _____

17. chopper _____

18. biggest _____

19. cutting _____

20. bigger _____

21. quitting _____

22. hopping _____

Suffixes and endings: Doubling the final consonant

HOME Name a base word and ask your child to spell the word with a suffix

Name_____

> Read each sentence. Add a suffix or ending to each word. Then circle the word that completes the sentence.

> **RULE**
> When a word ends in silent **e**, drop the e before adding a suffix or ending that begins with a vowel.
>
> take   tak**ing**
> large larg**est**

1.

May-ling _____ her music every afternoon.

practice + es = _____   close + es = _____

2.

Fluffy is the _____ cat I've ever seen!

ripe + est = _____   cute + est = _____

3.

Chef Edna _____ cucumbers for a salad.

trace + es = _____   slice + es = _____

4.

Dale makes up stories because she wants to

be a _____.

write + er = _____   dive + er = _____

5.

Mike has a job _____ leaves for his neighbor.

hide + ing = _____   rake + ing = _____

6.

Carlos _____ an insect for his science fair project.

examine + ed = _____   invite + ed = _____

Suffixes and endings: Words ending in e, Words in context   **107**

RULE
When a word ends in silent **e**, drop the **e** before adding **es**, **ed**, **ing**, or **est**.
hope   hop**ing**
large   larg**est**

Make new words by adding the suffixes or endings shown below. Write the new words in the correct columns.

	es	ed	ing
1. space	_____	_____	_____
2. race	_____	_____	_____
3. pose	_____	_____	_____
4. lace	_____	_____	_____
5. glaze	_____	_____	_____
6. place	_____	_____	_____
7. face	_____	_____	_____

	er	est
8. fine	_____	_____
9. ripe	_____	_____
10. cute	_____	_____
11. pure	_____	_____
12. tame	_____	_____
13. nice	_____	_____
14. late	_____	_____

HOME
Say a base word, then say a suffix or ending and ask your child to spell the new word.

Name_____

> **Write the base word for each word below.**

1. taking _____ 2. hiding _____

3. shining _____ 4. chased _____

5. bravest _____ 6. used _____

7. places _____ 8. baker _____

9. traced _____ 10. hoping _____

11. safer _____ 12. largest _____

> **Read each sentence. Circle the word that has a suffix or ending and write its base word on the line.**

13. Carl was shaking his bank. _____

14. "I need a larger baseball mitt," he said. _____

15. "I want the latest model." _____

16. Nothing rattled when he shook the bank. _____

17. He had spent almost all of his money on ice skates. _____

18. "I only practiced on them once," he said. _____

19. "Mom told me the lake seldom freezes." _____

20. Carl thought baseball was the finest game. _____

21. He could have used the mitt all summer. _____

22. "I should have been wiser," he said. _____

Read each sentence. Complete the sentence by adding the correct suffix or ending to the word in parentheses. Write the new word on the line.

1. Dan has a little brother _____ Tim.   (name)

2. Dan usually _____ to baby-sit with Tim.   (like)

3. One day Dan's parents _____ to go to a wedding. (arrange)

4. Dan had planned to go ice _____ that day.   (skate)

5. His parents _____ he'd baby-sit with Tim.   (hope)

6. Dan hated _____ his plans.   (change)

7. Then Mother had an idea that _____ the day.   (save)

8. "How about _____ Tim with you?" she asked.   (take)

9. Dan _____ that it was a good idea.   (agree)

10. "Taking Tim is _____ than not going," said Dan. (nice)

11. Tim was happy to be _____ along.   (invite)

12. "You'll be the _____ kid on skates!" said Dan. (cute)

13. They had the _____ weather for skating.   (fine)

14. The boys _____ swiftly over the ice.   (glide)

 What do you think happened next?

 Help your child think of sentences using words from the page to continue the story.

Name_____

Read the paragraphs. Then write the correct word on the line to complete each sentence.

The Dino Guide

My name is Rosa Gonzales. When I grow up I want to be just like my aunt Carmen! Aunt Carmen works in a natural history museum as a tour guide. That means she helps people understand the things they are looking at. My aunt's job is in the best part of the museum. She gives tours of the dinosaur exhibits. We call her the "Dino Guide."

Aunt Carmen says that the largest dinosaurs were more than 130 feet tall. They could have looked in the windows of a six-story building. My aunt is often invited to talk about dinosaurs at schools. She's been promising to bring a dinosaur egg to my class! She says the egg was found in a nest on the ground. It is only about 7 inches across. That is much smaller than I would expect a dinosaur's egg to be. Who could have thought that a dinosaur could begin its life inside an egg that size?

1. Aunt Carmen _____ in a natural history museum.

2. She helps people understand the things they are _____ at.

3. She gives _____ of the dinosaur exhibits.

4. The _____ dinosaurs were more than 130 feet tall.

5. They could have _____ in the windows of a six-story building.

6. She's been _____ to bring a dinosaur egg to my class.

7. The egg is only about 7 _____ across.

8. It is much _____ than I would expect.

 Do you think Aunt Carmen likes her job? Why or why not?

When you write in a diary, you are writing for yourself. You can make an entry in a diary when you want to remember things or express yourself. Writing a **diary entry** can also help you sort out your feelings or think about things that happened.

Imagine you are a travel writer. In your diary, describe some things you saw on your last trip. Some of the words in the box may help you.

traveling	writer	faster	days
monkeys	wolves	learned	cooking
worked	starting	bigger	coldest

Write the day or date at the beginning of your entry.

_____

_____

_____

Write about the **things you saw** and how you felt about them.

_____

_____

_____

_____

Remember you are writing for yourself.

_____

_____

_____

_____

HOME

Ask your child to read the diary page to you and identify the words with suffixes and endings.

Name _____

Read each sentence. Add the **suffix ful**, **less**, **y**, **ly**, or **ness** to the word below the line. Write the new word on the line.

> When a **suffix** is added at the end of a base word, it changes the base word's meaning or the way it is used.
>
> Hope**ful** means **full of hope**.
> Slow**ly** means **in a slow way**.
> Help**less** means **without help**.
> Sick**ness** means **being sick**.
> Bump**y** means **having bumps**.

1. Jan was sick, and food seemed _____ to her.
   (taste)

2. She was _____, but it was hard to swallow.
   (thirst)

3. "Your face is pale and looks _____," said Mother.
   (color)

4. "I hope the doctor can see you _____."
   (quick)

5. Jan's _____ turned out not to be serious.
   (ill)

6. "Medicine will help you," the doctor said _____.
   (kind)

7. "You must be _____ to get plenty of rest."
   (care)

8. "I don't like being sick," Jan said _____.
   (sad)

9. Mother gave her a _____ of medicine.
   (spoon)

10. Jan felt _____ and took a nap.
    (sleep)

What can Jan do to get better?

> **Read each word. Make new words by adding the suffixes. Write the new words in the correct columns.**

	y	**less**	**ful**
1. tear	_____	_____	_____
2. need	_____	_____	_____
3. fruit	_____	_____	_____
4. cheer	_____	_____	_____
5. trust	_____	_____	_____

	ly	**ness**
6. sick	_____	_____
7. neat	_____	_____
8. loud	_____	_____
9. quick	_____	_____
10. bright	_____	_____

> **Write the base word for each of the words below.**

11. kindness	_____	12. gladly	_____
13. tricky	_____	14. harmless	_____
15. spoonful	_____	16. rainy	_____
17. useful	_____	18. sadness	_____
19. homeless	_____	20. kindly	_____

HOME
Choose a base word and a suffix and ask your child to say the new word.

Name_____

► **Add the suffix to each word. Write the new words on the lines.**

> **RULE**
> The suffixes **ion** and **ment** form nouns. They usually mean "the condition of being." The suffix **ion** also means "the act of." Protect**ion** is the act of protecting. Excite**ment** is the condition of being excited.

ion

1. connect_____

2. attract _____

3. correct _____

4. select _____

ment

5. move _____

6. enjoy _____

7. pay _____

8. place _____

► **Read each sentence. Circle the word that correctly completes the sentence. Write the word on the line.**

9. Tom was waiting for the _____ of his new sled.

placement   shipment

10. To his _____, it came in a few days.

movement   amazement

11. Tom dressed for _____ against the weather.

protection   treatment

12. He placed the sled in just the right _____ .

connection   direction

13. The sled's _____ on the snow was terrific!

action   discussion

Suffixes: -ion, -ment, Words in context 115

▶ **Read each word and write its base word on the line beside it.**

1. washable _____

2. harden _____

3. darken _____

4. collectible _____

5. brighten _____

6. drivable _____

7. soften _____

8. sinkable _____

9. flexible _____

10. breakable _____

11. likable _____

12. lovable _____

▶ **Read each clue. Write the answer in the crossword puzzle.**

Across

1. to have good sense
4. it can be broken
6. it can be washed
7. to make something hard
8. to make something dark

Down

2. it can be sunk
3. to make something bright
5. it is liked

Ask your child to add new suffixes or endings to some of the base words in items 1–12.

Name_____

> **Read each base word and add the suffix. Write the new word on the line.**

1. move + ment _____

2. dark + en _____

3. invent + ion _____

4. like + able _____

5. pay + ment _____

6. fright + en _____

7. break + able _____

8. sense +ible _____

> **Fill in the circle beside the word that completes each sentence. Write the word on the line.**

9. Jill needed to _____ out her room.

○ harden   ○ straighten   ○ frighten

10. She began by sorting out her huge rock _____.

○ collection   ○ connection   ○ direction

11. Jill needed to get it down to a _____ size.

○ reversible   ○ flexible   ○ sensible

12. She made her _____ very carefully.

○ invention   ○ action   ○ selection

13. Then she found a _____ place to put the rocks.

○ suitable   ○ washable   ○ sinkable

14. Now, that was an _____!

○ payment   ○ improvement   ○ pavement

RULE
A suffix or ending that has one vowel sound forms a syllable by itself:

hard-en   **say**-ing

 Divide each word into syllables. Write the syllables on the lines.

1. playing _____

2. lighten _____

3. spoonful _____

4. gladly _____

5. needed _____

6. playful _____

7. cheerful _____

8. lovely _____

9. movement_____

10. loudest _____

11. useless _____

12. darkness _____

13. training _____

14. eating _____

15. homeless _____

16. shipment _____

17. careful _____

18. laughing _____

19. patches _____

20. painting _____

21. payment _____

22. snowy _____

23. hopeful _____

24. neatness _____

25. slowly _____

26. waiting _____

27. careless _____

28. rainy _____

29. brighten _____

30. useful _____

HOME Help your child think of sentences using words from the page.

Name_____

> In each box draw a line from the base word in the first column with a suffix in the second column to make a new word. Write the word on the line.

1.

luck   able   _____

cold   y   _____

wash   ion   _____

protect   est   _____

2.

fly   less   _____

loud   ing   _____

peach   est   _____

meat   es   _____

3.

safe   y   _____

pay   ing   _____

health   ly   _____

say   ment   _____

4.

teach   less   _____

home   ed   _____

land   ful   _____

cup   er   _____

5.

sink   y   _____

polite   ly   _____

cloud   en   _____

fright   able   _____

6.

sleep   ful   _____

light   ment   _____

spoon   y   _____

place   en   _____

7.

ax   ly   _____

sad   ible   _____

use   ful   _____

collect   es   _____

8.

fox   ed   _____

hammer   ness   _____

neat   able   _____

break   es   _____

Write the number of syllables in each word.

1. knives ___   2. plays ___   3. shelves ___

4. boxes ___   5. payment ___   6. tagging ___

7. cleaned ___   8. parties ___   9. jumped ___

10. hopeful ___   11. thirsty ___   12. loving ___

13. loudly ___   14. action ___   15. sleepy ___

16. painful ___   17. darken ___   18. sickness ___

19. receiving ___   20. foxes ___   21. shipment ___

22. wives ___   23. days ___   24. harmless ___

25. purest ___   26. sensible ___   27. leaves ___

28. shining ___   29. running ___   30. gladly ___

31. cherries ___   32. cooking ___   33. patches ___

34. begging ___   35. flexible ___   36. wolves ___

37. skated ___   38. weakest ___   39. snowy ___

40. straighten ___   41. homeless ___   42. smoothest ___

43. pavement ___   44. axes ___   45. correction ___

46. turkeys ___   47. whitest ___   48. sinkable ___

49. breakable ___   50. raking ___   51. daisies ___

HOME Say a word on the page and ask your child to name the syllables.

Name _____

Phonics & Spelling

Say and spell each word. Write the words on the note pad where they belong.

bushes	chopped	foxes	gives	losses
lunches	nicer	padded	pencils	pillows
running	saved	tagging	takes	writing

Plurals

_____

_____

_____

_____

_____

_____

Base Word with Final e

_____

_____

_____

_____

_____

Final Consonant Doubled Before Adding Ending

_____

_____

_____

_____

Pick a word from each column and write a complete sentence that uses the word.

1. _____

2. _____

3. _____

A **news story** tells people facts about something interesting that has happened. It gives readers the *who, what, when, where,* and *why* of an event. The writer gathers information by reading, observing things, or asking people interview questions.

> **Think of an interesting event in your school or community. Write the questions you would ask if you could interview someone who was involved in the event. Some of the words in the box may help you.**

quickly	it's	helping	you've
action	useful	started	what's
happened	longer	where's	latest

Write the name of the person you will interview.

Begin questions with words like *who, what, when, where,* and *why.*

Try to **avoid** questions that can be answered with a simple yes or no.

Name _____

Working in a Zoo

Would you like to work with animals every day? What if the animals were lions, elephants, tigers, monkeys, wolves, and giraffes? If you would enjoy that sort of work, you'd like being a zookeeper. Zookeepers take care of the animals that live in zoos. They do many different kinds of jobs.

1

FOLD

Zookeepers talk with people who visit the zoo. They tell them about the animals and how they live in the wild. They try to answer all of their questions.

Many zookeepers have studied animals in college. Some get their start working as volunteers at a zoo. Some zoos hire young people to work in the summer. Would you like to work in a zoo?

4

Zookeepers provide clean water and food for the animals. They must know what kind of food is best for each animal and just how much the animal should eat. They also care for the animals by brushing them, bathing them, and making sure they get enough exercise.

2

FOLD

Zookeepers make sure that the places where the animals live are clean and safe. The animals' homes must offer them protection from visitors and other animals. Zookeepers also watch the animals to be sure they're healthy. If an animal is sick, it must get treatment quickly.

3

Name _____

> **Circle the word that will finish each sentence. Write the word on the line.**

1. Our swim team _____ newspapers to raise money.　　collected　　collecting

2. We worked with other school _____ .　　team　　teams

3. People _____ their papers at the curb.　　places　　placed

4. We _____ up some yesterday.　　picker　　picked

5. Our swim _____ drove the truck.　　coach　　coached

6. It was a _____ day.　　wind　　windy

7. We _____ a lot of loose papers!　　chased　　chasing

8. We did better than we had _____ .　　hoped　　hopped

9. Today my dad is _____ the truck.　　drive　　driving

10. We already have fifty _____ of newspapers.　　box　　boxes

11. _____ keeping them in a garage.　　Were　　We're

12. Some boxes are _____ than others.　　bigger　　biggest

13. We have to be _____ lifting them.　　careful　　careless

14. Tomorrow _____ take them to be recycled.　　will　　we'll

Contractions, plurals, suffixes, endings: Assessment　　**125**

 Read the two words. Then fill in the circle beside the correct contraction.

1. you + will
   ○ you're   ○ you'll

2. will + not
   ○ we'll   ○ won't

3. here + is
   ○ he'll   ○ here's

4. we + have
   ○ we'll   ○ we've

5. does + not
   ○ doesn't   ○ don't

6. it + is
   ○ its   ○ it's

7. let + us
   ○ she's   ○ let's

8. I + have
   ○ I've   ○ I'll

9. we + will
   ○ we'll   ○ we've

10. can + not
    ○ won't   ○ can't

11. could + not
    ○ wouldn't   ○ couldn't

12. are + not
    ○ aren't   ○ can't

Read the word and the ending. Fill in the circle next to the correct spelling.

13. lily + s
    ○ lilys   ○ lilies

14. elf + s
    ○ elfs   ○ elves

15. quick + ness
    ○ quickness   ○ quickeness

16. rip + ed
    ○ ripped   ○ riped

17. skate + ing
    ○ skating   ○ skateing

18. rest + ed
    ○ restted   ○ rested

19. toy + s
    ○ toys   ○ toyes

20. glad + ly
    ○ gladly   ○ gladdly

21. smart + est
    ○ smartest   ○ smarttest

22. examine + ed
    ○ examined   ○ examineed

23. break + able
    ○ breakle   ○ breakable

24. protect + ion
    ○ protection   ○ protecton

Read Aloud

The Horse in the Sea

A strange and beautiful horse lives among the many fish that swim in the sea. Of course, sea horses aren't really horses, but they are a kind of fish.

The body of a sea horse is covered with hard, spiny plates that protect it. A long tail that wraps around seaweed or coral keeps the sea horse from floating away.

Sea horses can change color. Changing color helps a sea horse blend in with the background so it can't be seen by enemies.

TALK
About It

Do you think a sea horse is a good name for a fish? Tell why or why not.

Dear Family,

In this unit "By the Sea!" your child will learn to read and write words with vowel pairs (**oa** as in b**oa**t), vowel digraphs (**aw** as in cl**aw**), and diphthongs (**oi** as in c**oi**ns). As he or she explores words with these sounds, you might like to try these activities together.

▶ Help your child think of words about the sea that contain a vowel pair, vowel digraph, or diphthong, such as s**ea**l, fl**oa**t, h**oo**k, b**oa**t, b**ea**ch, s**ea** horse. Have your child draw a picture for each word. Then, write the word below the picture.

▶ Read the selection "The Horse in the Sea" on page 127. Help your child find words with vowel pairs, vowel digraphs, or diphthongs such as s**ea**, t**ai**l, and ar**ou**nd.

▶ Your child might enjoy reading these books with you. Look for them in your local library.

Coral Reef by Barbara Taylor
Eyewitness: Seashore by Steve Parker

Sincerely,

_____

Estimada familia:

En esta unidad titulada "By the Sea!", (A la orilla del mar) su hijo/a aprenderá a leer y escribir palabras en inglés con parejas de vocales (**oa**, como en b**oa**t), digramas de vocales (**aw**, como en cl**aw**) y diptongos (**oi**, como en c**oi**n). A medida que su hijo/a explore palabras con estos sonidos, quizás deseen hacer las siguientes actividades juntos.

▶ Ayuden a su hijo/a a pensar en palabras en inglés relacionadas con el mar que contengan una pareja de vocales, un digrama de vocales o un diptongo, tales como s**ea**l, fl**oa**t, h**oo**k, b**oa**t, b**ea**ch, s**ea** horse. Pídanle que haga un dibujo que ilustre cada palabra y que escriba la palabra debajo del dibujo.

▶ Lean la selección "The Horse in the Sea" (El caballo en el mar), en la página 127. Ayuden a su hijo/a a hallar palabras con parejas de vocales, digramas de vocales o diptongos, tales como s**ea**, t**ai**l y ar**ou**nd.

▶ Ustedes y su hijo/a disfrutarán leyendo estos libros juntos. Búsquenlos en su biblioteca local.

Coral Reef de Barbara Taylor

Eyewitness: Seashore de Steve Parker

Sinceramente,

_____

Name _____

In a vowel pair, two vowels come together to make one long vowel sound. When one syllable has a vowel pair, the first vowel stands for the long sound and the second vowel is silent.

true	boat	tree	pie
toe	leaf	train	tray

Read each sentence and underline the word with a vowel pair. Then, write the words on the lines at the bottom of the page.

1. Ann and Ted went to the stable to feed the horses.

2. The horses like to eat oats from the large pail.

3. Ann and Ted tried to ride at least once a week.

4. The plan for today was to go riding on the trail.

5. It was chilly, and the leaves were changing colors.

6. There were many pretty trees and bushes.

7. Ann and Ted stopped for lunch by a stream.

8. A toad jumped along the grassy bank.

9. Ann wiggled her toes in the cool water.

10. Ted lay on the grass and gazed at the blue sky.

11. A tiny boat with a red sail drifted by them.

_____   _____   _____

_____   _____   _____

_____   _____   _____

_____   _____   _____

_____   _____   _____

TALK About It

If Ann and Ted rode on the same trail three months later, what would they see?

Find the word in the box that will complete the sentence. Write the word on the line.

breeze	blue	day	leaves
paint	boat	feels	green
playing	tries	sea	Joe

1. Kay wants to _____ a picture today.

2. She decides to paint a picture of the _____.

3. First, she shows the water with the color _____.

4. Then, she draws some _____ sea plants.

5. The plants have long, green _____.

6. Next, she draws a _____ sailing on the sea.

7. The boat has a red sail to catch the _____.

8. Kay asks her friend _____ what to draw next.

9. Then, she _____ to think of some sea animals.

10. She decides to show two seals _____ in the sea.

11. Finally, Kay is finished for the _____.

12. She _____ proud of the picture she has made.

 What would you draw in a picture of the sea?

 Help your child make up a story about a day on the beach using the words in the box.

Name_____

> Read each sentence. Find the word or words from the box that best complete each sentence. Write each word on the line.

beach	day	tried	away
sailing	treat	cheese	Joe
boat	Sue	floated	sea gulls

1. It was a great _____ to go to the _____.

2. Mom made us _____ sandwiches for lunch.

3. After lunch, Grandma and I _____ to build a sand castle.

4. Later, the waves washed the sand castle _____.

5. Dean spotted some _____ flying.

6. My sister _____ spied some starfish on a rock.

7. Dad and _____ took the boat out _____.

8. They had to tow the _____ to shore after the wind stopped.

9. Grandpa _____ on a raft.

10. Going to the beach is a real _____ for my family!

What do you think you would like to do at the beach?

Vowel pairs ai, ay, ea, ee, ie, oa, oe, ue: Words in context, critical thinking   **131**

> Fill in the circle next to the word that completes the sentence. Write the word on the line.

1. Jason and Jeff _____ in the snow all day.   ○ plain   ○ played

2. Making a snowman made them _____ very cold.   ○ foam   ○ feel

3. They went inside to play with Jeff's _____.   ○ tree   ○ train

4. It felt good to remove their winter _____.   ○ coats   ○ coal

5. Jeff's dog wagged its _____ to greet them.   ○ tie   ○ tail

6. Jeff's mom made some hot apple cider for a _____.   ○ treat   ○ tried

7. They sat on the _____ carpet to play.   ○ blue   ○ blow

8. A _____ on the train came off the track.   ○ when   ○ wheel

9. Jason _____ to help Jeff fix it.   ○ tray   ○ tried

10. Soon it was able to _____ along the rails.   ○ coast   ○ crow

11. The train ran smoothly the rest of the _____.   ○ deal   ○ day

> Read each clue. Then write the answer that contains the given vowel pair.

12. something to sail in   oa   _____

13. something we do to shoelaces   ie   _____

14. something that runs on tracks   ai   _____

15. something on your foot   oe   _____

16. something we do at recess   ay   _____

17. something that grows on a tree   ea   _____

  Vowel pairs ai, ay, ea, ee, ie, oa, oe, ue:
Words in context

 HOME

Help your child think of other words with vowel pairs *oa, ie, ai, oe, ay, ea* such as *float, dried,* or *wait.*

Name_____

> Circle each word that has the vowel digraph **oo** or **ea**. Then write the words in the correct columns.

RULE

In a **vowel digraph**, two letters together stand for one vowel sound. It can be short or long, or have a special sound of its own. The vowel digraph **oo** stands for the vowel sound you hear in *book* and *pool*. The vowel digraph **ea** can stand for the short **e** sound you hear in *bread*.

1. Mike and Joe looked at the clock and saw that it was noon.

2. They stood up and left the classroom.

3. The weather was cool, so they grabbed their jackets.

4. They were ready to play a good game of football.

5. Mike threw the heavy ball, and it sailed over Joe's head.

6. The ball took a sudden turn toward the school wall.

7. Mike watched with dread as it went toward a window.

8. At the last minute, Joe scooped up the ball.

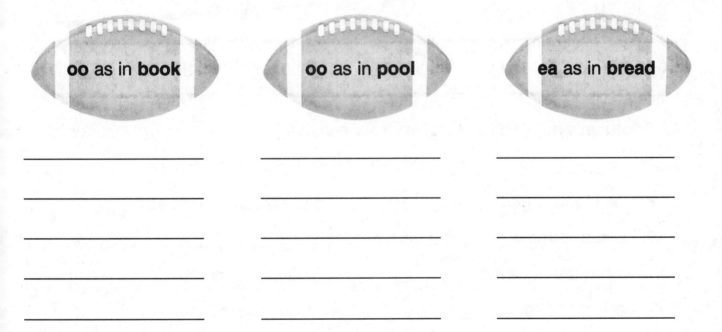

oo as in **book**   oo as in **pool**   ea as in **bread**

_____   _____   _____

_____   _____   _____

_____   _____   _____

_____   _____   _____

_____   _____   _____

What would the boys have done if they had broken a window?

Vowel digraphs oo, ea: Sound to symbol, critical thinking   **133**

Find the word in the box that will complete the sentence. Write the word on the line.

> **RULE**
> Sometimes, **ea** has a short **e** sound, as in *head*.

| bread | breakfast | headlines | heavy | ready | weather |

1. Heather and Sid eat a large _____ every day.

2. They have _____ and jam with their milk and cereal.

3. Sid reads all the _____ in the newspaper first.

4. The _____ report said that it would snow later.

5. Heather and Sid put on their _____ coats and boots.

6. Now they are _____ for their long walk to school.

Find the word in the box that will complete the sentence. Write the word on the line.

> **RULE**
> In most words **ei** has a long **a** sound, as in *eight*.

| eight | eighteen | neighbor | veins | weighs | weight |

7. Lauren's health class grew from sixteen to _____ students.

8. Her _____, Mrs. Parkhurst, is the health teacher.

9. She teaches that _____ carry blood to the heart.

10. Lauren learns how to read a scale to find her _____.

11. It shows that Lauren _____ sixty pounds.

12. Lauren gained _____ pounds since last year.

HOME Have your child make up sentences using the words in the boxes such as, *Dan is ready for breakfast.*

> **RULE**
>
> The vowel digraphs **aw** and **au** have the sound you hear in *saw* and *caught*. The vowel digraph **ei** can have the long **a** sound you hear in *eight*.

Circle each word that has the vowel digraph **aw**, **au**, or **ei**. Then write the words in the correct columns below.

1. Shaun sat on the lawn under a tree and yawned.

2. The August sun made him sleepy, and his book felt like a heavy weight.

3. He watched an ant crawl up a vein on a leaf.

4. He heard a neighing sound from his neighbor's horse.

5. He dreamed he was drawing an awesome dinosaur.

6. His art teacher had taught him how to sketch them.

7. The whistle of a freight train caught his attention, and he woke up.

aw as in **saw**	**au** as in **caught**	**ei** as in **eight**
_____	_____	_____
_____	_____	_____
_____	_____	_____
_____	_____	_____

Circle each word that has a vowel digraph. Then, write the words in the correct column.

1. In August Paul mowed the lawn at his uncle's big farm.

2. He liked to start in the morning when it was cool.

3. Sometimes he hauled bales of straw to the barn.

4. His uncle often helped him lift the heavy load.

5. During the hot afternoon, his head began to sweat.

6. He met his neighbors at the swimming pool.

7. Before diving, he looked for the deepest water.

8. By eight o'clock he was so tired that he began to yawn.

9. He went home to read a good book about weight lifting.

(oo as in **book**)	(oo as in **moon**)	(ei as in **sleigh**)
_____	_____	_____
_____	_____	_____
_____	_____	_____

(ea as in **thread**)	(aw as in **saw**)	(au as in **auto**)
_____	_____	_____
_____	_____	_____
_____	_____	_____

 Do you think Paul likes to work on the farm? Why or why not?

 With your child, look in a newspaper for words that contain the vowel digraphs oo, *ei, ea, aw,* and *au.*

Vowel digraphs oo, ei, ea, aw, au: Sound to symbol, critical thinking

Name_____

▶ Read the clues. Find the word that matches each clue.
Write the word in the puzzle.

brook	eel	eight	snail	seaweed
coast	sailfish	prawn	sea horse	sawfish

Across

2. a food from the sea that is like a shrimp
5. a fish with a long slippery body
6. a slow-moving sea animal with a coiled shell
8. the number after seven
9. a small fish with a head like a horse

Down

1. a small stream
3. a large fish with a big fin
4. the land along the sea
7. a large member of the ray family with a saw-like snout
10. one of many kinds of water plants

Vowel pairs and digraphs: Word meaning   **137**

In the sentences below, underline each word that contains a vowel pair or a vowel digraph. Write the words in the correct columns.

1. The freezing rain and sleet beat on our gray home.

2. The streets looked awfully icy for a March day.

3. The news said a blue bus was caught in a ditch.

4. The news headline said, "No school today because of heavy snow."

5. The weather wasn't good for a sleigh ride.

6. My mother said that I could play with my neighbor, Kay.

7. I helped Mom bake raisin bread instead.

8. We feel that it is easy to have fun.

Vowel Pair	Vowel Digraph
_____	_____
_____	_____
_____	_____
_____	_____
_____	_____
_____	_____
_____	_____
_____	_____
_____	_____
_____	_____
_____	_____
_____	_____

Have your child write a short story using as many words with vowel pairs or digraphs as he or she is able to.

Name _____

Read the journal entry. Then, write words with vowel pairs and vowel digraphs to complete each sentence.

Gentle Giants
February 14

Our sightseeing boat floated deep in the blue waters of the lagoon. Within a short time, we spotted our first gray whale. This 40-foot giant was bigger than I could imagine! We were told they can weigh as much as 35 tons. We soon began to see one whale after another. The whales seemed very playful and curious. A friendly mother whale and her calf swam up to our boat to get a closer look at us. Suddenly, they dove into the water. When they burst up again, they spouted water. It felt like rain, and we got awfully wet. I learned that gray whales have two blowholes that help them to breathe. After seeing these beautiful animals up close, I understand why it is so important to take care of our oceans and respect all animals.

1. Our boat _____ deep in the waters of the blue _____.

2. We soon spotted our first 40-foot _____ whale.

3. These gentle animals seemed very _____ and curious.

4. A gray whale can _____ as much as 35 tons.

5. A friendly mother whale and her calf swam close to our _____ to get a closer _____ at us.

6. We got _____ wet when the whales spouted water.

7. Gray whales have two blowholes to help them _____.

Why do you think it is so important to keep our oceans clean?

Review vowel pairs and digraphs: Reading, critical thinking   **139**

Phonics & Writing

A **friendly letter** helps us stay in touch with people we care about. We can share news, tell our feelings, or cheer a friend. We use words that are fun and friendly to tell about what we are doing.

▶ **Imagine you are spending a day by the sea. Write a friendly letter to tell someone about the sights you saw and the things you did. Some of the words in the box may help you.**

blue	coast	eight	floated	green
looked	play	ready	saw	tried

The **greeting** usually begins with Dear and the person's name.

The **heading** tells the date.

The **body**, or main part, tells about things you did.

End with a **closing**, such as Your friend, and your name.

HOME Invite your child to read his or her friendly letter aloud.

Name _____

A **diphthong** consists of two letters blended together to make one vowel sound.

oy=oi	ow=ou
boy boil	owl scout

ew
stew

> Circle the word that completes each sentence. Write the word on the line.

1. A team of scientists traveled to the _____ Pole.   South   Soil

2. They wanted to explore _____ places.   now   new

3. They asked a photographer to _____ them.   jewel   join

4. Everyone rejoiced when their goal _____ near.   drew   blow

5. They _____ they had succeeded.   know   knew

6. At first, the only _____ they heard was the wind.   screw   sound

7. They wore face masks when the wind _____.   blow   blew

8. They fell _____ on the ice and snow.   dew   down

9. Sometimes they had to _____ to each other.   shout   show

10. They had to _____ snow to cook their food.   boil   boy

11. Often they ate canned _____.   stew   slow

12. Everyone _____ tired and cold.   ground   grew

13. A chance to rest was cause for _____.   joy   join

14. One day they heard a group of _____ seals.   noisy   choice

15. They saw a whale leap _____ of the water.   out   mouth

16. It blew air and water out of its _____.   spoil   spout

17. The water looked like a _____.   fountain   found

 Why do you think the scientists traveled so far?

Diphthongs oy, oi, ow, ou, ew: Words in context, critical thinking 141

Read each clue. Choose the word from the box that matches the clue, and write it on the line. Circle the diphthong in each word you write.

1. a form of money _____

2. drops of water on the grass at night _____

3. things that children like to play with _____

4. a place where people can live _____

5. the shape of a circle_____

6. a large number of people _____

7. what a ball can do _____

8. a headpiece for a king or queen _____

9. an animal from which we get milk _____

bounce	flowers
boy	house
cloud	mouse
coins	mouth
cow	owl
crowd	round
crown	stew
dew	toys

 Say the name of each picture. Choose the word from the box at the top of the page that names the picture, and write it on the line. Circle the diphthong.

10.

_____

11.

_____

12.

_____

13.

_____

14.

_____

15.

_____

 HOME

Ask your child to name words with the same diphthong as the picture words.

Name _____

> Read each word. On the first line, write the number of vowels you see. Say each word. On the second line, write the number of vowel sounds you hear. On the third line, write the number of syllables in the word.

AEIOU	Vowels You See	Vowel Sounds You Hear	Number of Syllables	AEIOU	Vowels You See	Vowel Sounds You Hear	Number of Syllables
1. autumn	___	___	___	17. measure	___	___	___
2. shook	___	___	___	18. instead	___	___	___
3. bread	___	___	___	19. neighborly	___	___	___
4. weigh	___	___	___	20. naughty	___	___	___
5. broom	___	___	___	21. headline	___	___	___
6. sweater	___	___	___	22. brook	___	___	___
7. bookcase	___	___	___	23. pause	___	___	___
8. school	___	___	___	24. eighteen	___	___	___
9. reindeer	___	___	___	25. leather	___	___	___
10. spool	___	___	___	26. haunted	___	___	___
11. sleigh	___	___	___	27. freight	___	___	___
12. feather	___	___	___	28. coins	___	___	___
13. bedspread	___	___	___	29. because	___	___	___
14. weighted	___	___	___	30. woodpile	___	___	___
15. woodpecker	___	___	___	31. raccoon	___	___	___
16. laundry	___	___	___	32. heavy	___	___	___

> Say the name of the picture at the beginning of each row, and look at the letters circled in the picture name. Circle the same pair of letters in each word in the row. Then write the number of syllables in the word on the line.

1.

st(ew)

st e w	___	c h e w y	___
f e w	___	c r e w	___
j e w e l r y	___	t h r e w	___

2.

c(oi)n s

p o i n t e r	___	v o i c e	___
b r o i l	___	j o i n	___
o i l c a n	___	s p o i l i n g	___

3.

t(oy)s

b o y	___	e n j o y	___
a n n o y	___	T r o y	___
r o y a l	___	t o y	___

4.

s c(ou)t

m o u s e	___	s h o u t e d	___
b o u n c e	___	c l o u d y	___
o u t s i d e	___	h o u s e	___

5.

(ow)l

c r o w n	___	n o w	___
u p t o w n	___	b r o w n	___
f r o w n s	___	f l o w e r p o t	___

Name_____

Phonics & Spelling

Feed each water animal words with the same vowel sound as its name. In the box, write the number of syllables or "bites" the animal gets with each word.

trout

1. _____ ☐

2. _____ ☐

3. _____ ☐

4. _____ ☐

crayfish

5. _____ ☐

6. _____ ☐

7. _____ ☐

8. _____ ☐

9. _____ ☐

eel

10. _____ ☐

11. _____ ☐

12. _____ ☐

chinook

13. _____ ☐

14. _____ ☐

praw**n**

15. _____ ☐

16. _____ ☐

hammerhea**d**

17. _____ ☐

18. _____ ☐

oyster

19. _____ ☐

20. _____ ☐

bluefish

21. _____ ☐

22. _____ ☐

23. _____ ☐

about	
autumn	
bay	
beaver	
boy	
bread	
cookies	
crawl	
cloud	
eight	
feel	
shout	
instead	
jewelry	
join	
neighborly	
owl	
paint	
pool	
sailor	
stew	
woodpecker	
greeting	

An **informative paragraph** gives facts about a topic. One sentence tells the main idea. Other sentences tell details about the main idea.

Think about a real or make-believe sea creature, and write an informative paragraph about it. Some of the words in the box may help you.

about	autumn	boy	bread	bay
crawl	dried	eight	feel	float
join	owl	paint	pool	stew

Include the **main idea** in your first sentence.

Include **details** about the main idea in the other sentences.

HOME Ask your child to read the story he or she wrote.

OCTOPUSES

An octopus is an unusual animal that lives in the sea. The octopus has eight arms, or tentacles. Each arm has two rows of suckers. There are about 250 suckers on each arm. An octopus uses its suckers to catch food. It then pulls its food into its mouth using its tentacles. The mouth of the octopus is pointed and hard like the beak of a bird.

FOLD

An octopus has two large eyes and sees very well. When an octopus sees an enemy, it can change color to try to blend in with its background. An octopus also changes color to show its mood. Brown is its usual color. When an octopus turns white, it is usually afraid. When it turns red, it is usually angry.

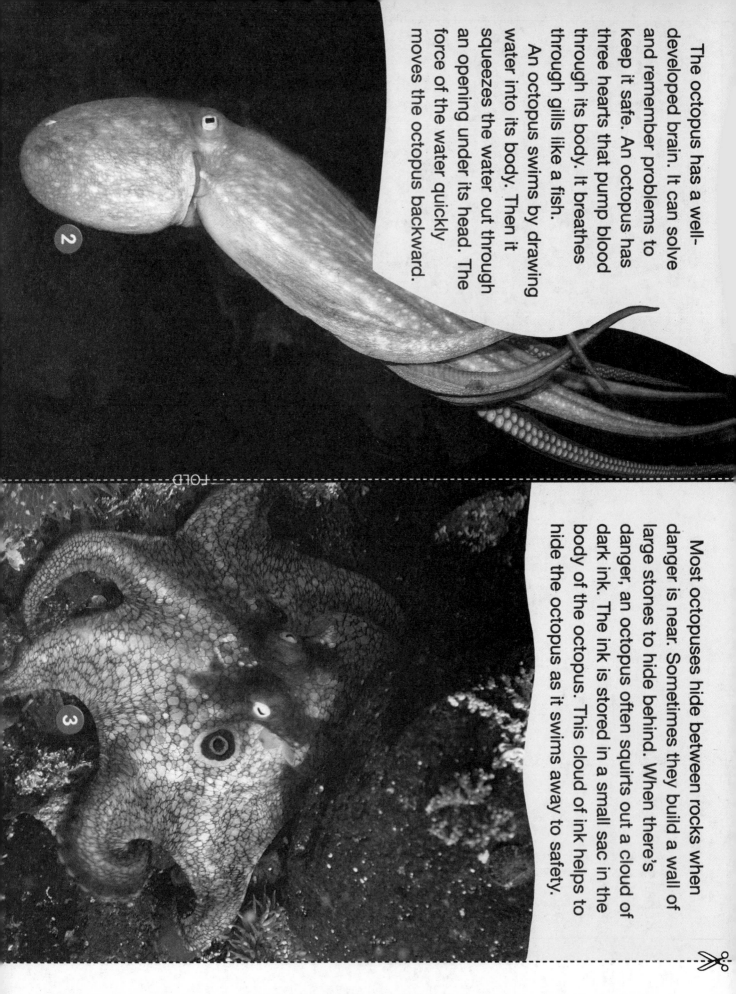

The octopus has a well-developed brain. It can solve and remember problems to keep it safe. An octopus has three hearts that pump blood through its body. It breathes through gills like a fish.

An octopus swims by drawing water into its body. Then it squeezes the water out through an opening under its head. The force of the water quickly moves the octopus backward.

2

Most octopuses hide between rocks when danger is near. Sometimes they build a wall of large stones to hide behind. When there's danger, an octopus often squirts out a cloud of dark ink. The ink is stored in a small sac in the body of the octopus. This cloud of ink helps to hide the octopus as it swims away to safety.

3

Review vowel pairs, digraphs, dipthongs: Take-home book

Name_____

> Read the word in the box. Fill in the circle in front
> of the word that has the same vowel sound.

1. awning

○ meat   ○ school   ○ taught

2. bread

○ led   ○ sea   ○ say

3. goose

○ scout   ○ tool   ○ book

4. weigh

○ feel   ○ boil   ○ late

5. clown

○ paid   ○ loud   ○ boat

6. boast

○ room   ○ chew   ○ goat

7. green

○ teach   ○ bread   ○ vein

8. joy

○ jaw   ○ join   ○ wood

9. pause

○ lawn   ○ eight   ○ leap

10. soak

○ shout   ○ soy   ○ toe

11. play

○ main   ○ crawl   ○ boy

12. mouse

○ crook   ○ broom   ○ brown

13. leaves

○ trees   ○ vein   ○ threw

14. good

○ boil   ○ bloom   ○ look

15. sail

○ stay   ○ draw   ○ tried

16. coin

○ toy   ○ shook   ○ soon

 Circle the word that best completes each sentence. Write the word on the line.

1. My brother and I _____ a riddle game.   played   plowed

2. We _____ turns making up animal riddles.   took   tied

3. What has a curly tail and says _____?   oats   oink

4. What is big and gray and _____
   up to 35 tons?   wait   weighs

5. What can fly and says _____?   chime   cheep

6. What is a large black bird that makes a sound

   like _____?   caw   coo

7. What is small, yellow and says _____?   paw   peep

8. What gives milk and makes a _____ sound?   may   moo

9. What can you sit on that runs fast and makes a

   _____ sound?   neigh   need

10. What sees well at night and can _____?   cool   hoot

11. What is soft and quiet and says _____?   mew   mow

12. What is cute and furry and eats fish for _____? mean   meals

13. "I _____ it's a cat," I said.   feel   feet

14. "No," he laughed. "It's a _____!"   south   seal

Read Aloud

The BOTTLE Houses

Everyone knows that it's important to recycle. Rather than wastefully throwing away things such as shopping bags or plastic containers, people try to reuse them. The Bottle Houses in Prince Edward Island, Canada, show a creative way to use things that might be thrown out.

The Bottle Houses are three buildings made of more than 25,000 glass bottles. They were built in the 1980s by a man named Edouard Arsenault (Ed-WAHRD Ar-seh-NOH).

Arsenault collected used bottles from many people and places. He used cement to hold the bottles together. Because the bottles are all different colors, the houses are very beautiful to look at, especially from the inside. Visitors enjoy taking pictures of the unusual houses. People might also come away with new ideas for recycling!

TALK about It If you could make something new from recycled objects, what would it be?

Dear Family,

In this unit about "Taking Care of Our Earth," your child will learn to identify prefixes, such as **un-** in **un**like, and suffixes, such as **-ness** in kind**ness**. Your child will also learn the rules for dividing words into syllables. As your child becomes familiar with these skills, you might like to try these activities together.

▶ With your child, look through favorite stories and magazines for words that begin with a prefix or end with a suffix.

▶ Read the article on page 151 with your child. Ask him or her to identify the words with prefixes and suffixes. Then help your child to think up something new that could be made from recycled objects. Ask him or her to draw a picture to illustrate the idea or, if practical, to create it.

▶ Your child might enjoy reading these books with you. Look for them in your local library.

Miss Rumphius
by Barbara Cooney

And Still the Turtle Watched
by Sheila MacGill-Callahan

Sincerely,

_____

Estimada familia:

En esta unidad, que trata sobre "Taking Care of Our Earth" ("Cuidemos nuestra Tierra"), su hijo/a aprenderá a identificar prefijos, como **un-** en **un**like, y sufijos, como **-ness** en kind**ness**. También aprenderá las reglas para dividir las palabras en sílabas. A medida que su hijo/a se vaya familiarizando con estas destrezas, pueden hacer las siguientes actividades juntos.

▶ Con su hijo/a, busquen en revistas y cuentos favoritos palabras que comienzan con un prefijo o terminan en un sufijo.

▶ Lean juntos el artículo en la página 151. Pidan a su hijo/a que identifique las palabras con prefijos y con sufijos. Después, ayúdenlo/a a crear algo nuevo que pueda construirse a partir de objetos reciclados. Pídanle que haga un dibujo para ilustrar su idea o, si resulta posible, que lo construya.

▶ Ustedes y su hijo/a disfrutarán leyendo estos libros juntos. Búsquenlos en su biblioteca local.

Miss Rumphius
de Barbara Cooney

And Still the Turtle Watched
de Sheila MacGill-Callahan

Sinceramente,

_____

Name_____

> **Read each word and write its base word on the line.**

A **prefix** is a word part that is added at the beginning of a base word to change the base word's meaning or the way it is used.
Dishonest means **not honest**.
Unbuckled means **not buckled**.
Misplaced means **not in the right place**.
Improper means **not proper**.
Inactive means **not active**.

1. displease _____

2. incorrect _____

3. impure _____

4. misbehave _____

5. unfair _____

6. unhappy _____

7. dissatisfy _____

8. unfold _____

9. disagree _____

10. misfortune _____

11. mislay _____

12. unpleasant _____

13. disobey _____

14. imperfect _____

15. discharge _____

16. uncover _____

17. misspell _____

18. imprecise _____

19. disappear _____

20. unseen _____

21. misuse _____

22. inaction _____

23. untrue _____

24. disable _____

25. mistake _____

26. uneven _____

27. dislike _____

28. incomplete _____

Read each word and write its base word on the line.

1. unable _____

2. unpleasant _____

3. unhappy _____

4. unmade _____

5. incorrect _____

6. misprint _____

7. dislike _____

8. improper _____

9. displease _____

10. impossible _____

 Read each sentence. Write a word from the examples above that means the same as the underlined words in the sentence.

11. Susan's mother thinks messy bedrooms are not proper. _____

12. Susan's bed was not made yesterday morning. _____

13. Susan was not able to clean her room before school. _____

14. Her mom was not happy and asked Susan to clean it. _____

15. Susan would not like making her mother angry. _____

16. She cleaned the not pleasant mess. _____

17. Susan knows it's not correct to leave her room messy. _____

Prefixes: im-, in-, un-, dis-, and mis-

 With your child, look up words in the dictionary with the prefixes *im-*, *in-*, *un-*, *dis-*, and *mis-*.

Name_____

 Read each word and write its base word on the line.

1. prepay _____

2. reread _____

3. defrost _____

4. exchange _____

5. express _____

6. rebuild _____

7. refill _____

8. derail _____

9. reopen _____

10. rewrite _____

11. preview _____

12. redo _____

13. preshrunk _____

14. depart _____

15. rewash _____

16. preschool _____

17. exclaim _____

18. detour _____

19. decode _____

20. export _____

21. preset _____

22. deplane _____

23. reteach _____

24. demerit _____

25. rewrap _____

26. reclaim _____

27. retie _____

28. decrease _____

▶ **Read each word and write its base word on the line.**

1. prepaid _____   5. mistake _____

2. retell _____   6. exclaim _____

3. unable _____   7. inactive _____

4. dishonest _____   8. depart _____

▶ **Fill in the circle beside the word that completes each sentence. Write the word on the line.**

9. Al _____ Marie's invitation.

○ reloaded   ○ reread   ○ refilled

10. He was _____ if he could go to the party.

○ unsure   ○ unsaid   ○ unsafe

11. He _____ ice cream and cake.

○ disagreed   ○ disowned   ○ disliked

12. He would go to the party, but he would

_____ early.

○ defend   ○ depart   ○ defrost

13. At the party Marie _____ her gifts.

○ unchained   ○ unloaded   ○ unwrapped

14. She could hardly wait to _____ the bows.

○ untie   ○ unpaid   ○ untrue

15. Al decided it would be _____ to leave early.

○ impure   ○ imperfect   ○ improper

HOME
Say a prefix (im-, in-, un-, dis-, mis-, ex-, de-, re-, pre-) to your child. Ask him or her to name a word with that prefix.

Name_____

Read the definitions carefully. Then read each word below, and write its prefix, its base word, and its suffix or ending, in the correct columns.

A **base word** is a word to which a prefix, suffix, or ending may be added to form a new word. A **prefix** is added at the beginning of a base word. A **suffix** or **ending** is added at the end of a base word.

re + turn = return

quick + **ly** = quickly

	prefix	base word	suffix or ending
1. rebuilding	____	_____	____
2. prepaying	____	_____	____
3. unkindly	____	_____	____
4. uncomfortable	____	_____	____
5. unhappiness	____	_____	____
6. incorrectly	____	_____	____
7. misbehaving	____	_____	____
8. displeasing	____	_____	____
9. unpacking	____	_____	____
10. exclaiming	____	_____	____
11. derailed	____	_____	____
12. repainting	____	_____	____
13. recycling	____	_____	____
14. immovable	____	_____	____
15. defrosting	____	_____	____

Read each sentence. Use the code to make the two words under the sentence. Then circle the word that completes the sentence. Underline the prefix, the suffix, or the ending in each of the coded words. Some words have a prefix and a suffix or an ending.

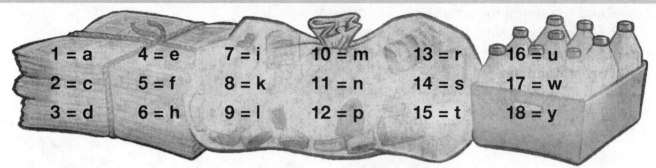

1 = a	4 = e	7 = i	10 = m	13 = r	16 = u
2 = c	5 = f	8 = k	11 = n	14 = s	17 = w
3 = d	6 = h	9 = l	12 = p	15 = t	18 = y

1. Let's all try to be _____ caretakers of our planet!

   __ __ __ __ __ __ __ __   __ __ __ __ __ __ __
   2 1 13 4 9 4 14 14   6 4 9 12 5 16 9

2. Try to _____ shopping bags and plastic containers.

   __ __ __ __ __ __ __   __ __ __ __ __
   3 7 14 9 7 8 4   13 4 16 14 4

3. Pick up _____ newspapers, bottles, and boxes and recycle them.

   __ __ __ __ __ __   __ __ __ __ __ __ __ __ __
   8 7 11 3 9 18   16 11 2 9 1 7 10 4 3

4. Try not to be _____ when using water or electricity.

   __ __ __ __ __ __ __ __   __ __ __ __ __ __ __ __
   17 1 14 15 4 5 16 9   13 4 5 7 9 9 4 3

5. If people _____ say they cannot help, share these tips.

   __ __ __ __ __ __   __ __ __ __ __ __ __ __
   11 4 1 15 9 18   16 11 17 7 14 4 9 18

HOME Using the code on the page, ask your child to make up words for you to decode.

Name_____

Divide each word into syllables.
Remember to use hyphens.

1. rewrite _____

2. movement _____

3. untie _____

4. dislike _____

5. unpaid _____

6. playing _____

7. spoonful _____

8. colder _____

9. softest _____

10. inside _____

11. unsafely _____

12. repainted _____

13. distasteful _____

14. unhandy _____

15. mistrust _____

16. renew _____

17. displease _____

18. premix _____

19. amazement _____

20. sleepless _____

21. boxes _____

22. dampness _____

23. rested _____

24. flying _____

25. unwisely _____

26. returning _____

27. improve _____

28. retelling _____

29. replanted _____

30. unkindly _____

31. excitement _____

32. departing _____

Study each rule about dividing words into syllables.

A one-syllable word is never divided.
house
Divide a compound word between the words that make up the compound word.

dog-house

Divide each compound word into syllables. Remember to use hyphens.

1. into _____

2. doorman _____

3. birthday _____

4. cowboy _____

5. rainbow _____

6. inside _____

7. tiptoe _____

8. someone _____

9. sidewalk _____

10. sunshine _____

11. tonight _____

12. today _____

13. dishpan _____

14. highway _____

15. moonlight _____

16. bedtime _____

17. weekend _____

18. headline _____

19. dustpan _____

20. hillside _____

21. sailboat _____

22. driveway _____

Challenge your child to think of more compound words and divide them into syllables.

Name_____

Downtown or Trash Town?

When is a city sidewalk like a trash can? When it has litter on it! Old newspapers, candy wrappers, soda cans, and other garbage make it look as if nobody cares about the place. That is what has happened to this city's downtown. The ugly mess cannot be overlooked.

Why don't people take better care of our outside areas? Litter not only is ugly, but also can turn into something unhealthy. Decaying litter and trash attracts animals that can carry disease.

You can help your hometown with this problem. Organize a litter drive. Get everyone together to make a difference in a park or playground, uptown or downtown, or along the highway.

1. A city _____ can look like a trash can.

2. Litter makes it look as if _____ cares.

3. The ugly mess _____ be _____.

4. Litter can turn into _____ that is very unhealthy.

5. You can help your _____ solve its litter problem.

6. Get _____ involved by having a litter drive.

 TALK About It What can you do to help prevent litter?

A **postcard** is a quick and easy way to send a message. The message should be short and to the point. One sentence should tell the main idea. The other sentences should tell details about the main idea.

Write a postcard to the mayor of your town and give three reasons why it is important to organize a litter drive. Some of the words in the box may help you.

downtown	anytime	backyard	cannot	citywide
weekend	somewhere	springtime	daylong	everyone

Write toda date at th top of you postcard.

Dear _____ ,

Put the **reason** for writing in your first sentence.

_____

_____

_____

_____

Write your ideas in the other sentences.

_____

_____

Sincerely,

_____

Don't forge **sign** your name.

Name_____

Study the rule. Then divide each word into syllables. Remember to use hyphens.

1. saying _____
2. sharpen _____
3. boxful _____
4. cheated _____
5. making _____
6. planted _____
7. pavement _____
8. homeless _____
9. needed _____
10. walking _____
11. newest _____
12. flying _____
13. cupful _____
14. kindly _____
15. playing _____
16. quicker _____

17. foxes _____
18. sleeping _____
19. safely _____
20. treatment _____
21. fearless _____
22. smallest _____
23. reading _____
24. gladly _____
25. helpless _____
26. healthful _____
27. rested _____
28. careless _____
29. colder _____
30. loudest _____
31. neatly _____
32. faster _____

Divide the words into syllables, using hyphens.

1. painful _____

2. tallest _____

3. playful _____

4. scary _____

5. watching _____

6. sickness _____

7. smarter _____

8. darted _____

9. loudly _____

10. classes _____

11. learning _____

12. singing _____

Read each sentence. Choose one of the words above to complete the sentence. Write it on the line.

13. Two _____ from our school visited the zoo.

14. We had fun _____ the animals.

15. One _____ monkey chased another.

16. The birds were _____ joyfully.

17. A lion roared _____

18. Otters _____ down a waterfall.

19. The alligator showed his _____ sharp teeth.

20. We enjoyed _____ new facts.

21. The _____ animal is the giraffe.

22. The elephant is _____ than most animals.

 HOME

Help your child use the words from numbers 1–12 in sentences.

Name _____

Study the rule. Then write each word, dividing it into syllables.

1. unable _____
2. reread _____
3. distrust _____
4. impure _____
5. depart _____
6. express _____
7. misprint _____
8. return _____
9. disown _____
10. untie _____
11. replace _____
12. exclaim _____
13. undress _____
14. premade _____
15. unkind _____
16. display _____

17. inform _____
18. misfit _____
19. exchange _____
20. unfair _____
21. preheat _____
22. displease _____
23. import _____
24. unscrew _____
25. derail _____
26. renew _____
27. export _____
28. repaint _____
29. discharge _____
30. unfold _____
31. input _____
32. defrost _____

Divide the words into syllables using hyphens.

1. unable   _____

2. discomfort _____

3. repair   _____

4. pregame   _____

5. remove   _____

6. delay   _____

7. depart   _____

8. request   _____

9. displease _____

10. unlock   _____

 Read each sentence. Choose one of the words above to complete the sentence. Write it on the line.

11. Beth used a key to _____ her trunk.

12. She had to _____ her suitcases.

13. She felt some _____ because of her heavy bag.

14. Beth had to _____ some help.

15. She was late because her car had needed

   a _____ .

16. Beth hadn't expected this _____ in her plans.

17. She hoped she would make the _____ show.

18. It would _____ Beth to miss the show.

19. Beth planned to _____ tomorrow.

20. She was _____ to stay longer.

 HOME Ask your child to name other words with prefixes to divide into syllables.

Name _____

> **Study the rule. Then write each word, dividing it into syllables.**

1. picture _____
2. pencil _____
3. confess _____
4. goblin _____
5. forgave _____
6. basket _____
7. admire _____
8. princess _____
9. complete _____
10. mistake _____
11. candy _____
12. harbor _____
13. plenty _____
14. children _____
15. pilgrim _____
16. sudden _____

17. number _____
18. silver _____
19. Kansas _____
20. master _____
21. finger _____
22. invite _____
23. kidnap _____
24. doctor _____
25. riddle _____
26. almost _____
27. chapter _____
28. surprise _____
29. dictate _____
30. butter _____
31. window _____
32. problem _____

Write each word, dividing it into syllables.

1. magnet _____
2. sudden _____
3. blanket _____
4. plenty _____
5. invite _____
6. hungry _____

7. circus _____
8. confess _____
9. picnic _____
10. almost _____
11. puppy _____
12. bottom _____

Read each sentence. Choose one of the words from above to complete the sentence. Write it on the line.

13. Dad and Meg took a delicious _____ to the park.

14. They laid the food on a _____.

15. They had _____ of food to eat.

16. There was a _____ tug on Meg's pants.

17. A _____ was pulling on them.

18. Meg _____ fell over.

19. The puppy was very _____, too.

20. Meg and Dad decided to _____ it to lunch.

Syllables: Words with two or more consonants between two vowels

HOME Help your child think of sentences using words from the page to continue the story.

Name _____

RULE

▶ **Read the rule. Then write each word, dividing it into syllables.**

> When a single consonant comes between two vowels in a word, the word is usually divided after the consonant if the first vowel is short.
> **lem-on**

1. robin _____

2. cabin _____

3. figure _____

4. wagon _____

5. travel _____

6. palace _____

7. statue _____

8. finish _____

9. river _____

10. clever _____

11. cover _____

12. visit _____

13. shadow _____

14. model _____

15. dozen _____

▶ **Write a paragraph that tells about the picture. Try to use some of the words in numbers 1–15.**

_____

_____

_____

_____

_____

_____

▶ **Write each word, dividing it into syllables.**

1. cabin   _____

2. travel   _____

3. magic   _____

4. visit   _____

5. figure   _____

6. palace   _____

7. ever   _____

8. river   _____

9. wagon   _____

10. clever   _____

▶ **Read each sentence. Choose one of the words in numbers 1–10 to complete the sentence. Write it on the line.**

11. There once lived a very _____ cat.

12. He lived in a tiny log _____.

13. He liked to _____ to many places.

14. One day he set off with his red _____.

15. When he got to a _____, he swam across.

16. He came to the royal _____.

17. "I think I shall _____ the king," he said.

18. "I'll do some _____ tricks for him."

19. The king could not _____ out how the tricks were done.

20. He wondered if the cat would

_____ visit him again.

170   Syllables: v-c-v words

Say *CA-bin*, *CAB-in*, pausing between syllables. Ask your child to identify the correct way to divide the syllables (*cab-in*). Repeat with *figure* (*fig-ure*), *palace* (*pal-ace*), and *ever* (*ev-er*).

Name _____

RULE

When a single consonant comes between two vowels in a word, the word is usually divided before the consonant if the first vowel is long.

ti-ny

▶ **Study the rule. Then write each word, dividing it into syllables.**

1. lilac _____

2. polar _____

3. spider _____

4. frozen _____

5. moment _____

6. lazy _____

7. pupil _____

8. lady _____

9. pirate _____

10. pilot _____

11. cozy _____

12. motel _____

13. David _____

14. music _____

15. tiger _____

16. broken _____

17. famous _____

18. paper _____

▶ **Write a sentence using some of the words in numbers 1–18.**

_____

_____

_____

_____

Write each word, dividing it into syllables.

1. paper _____

2. frozen _____

3. lilac _____

4. cozy _____

5. music _____

6. policeman _____

7. spider _____

8. pony _____

9. sofa _____

10. lazy _____

11. grocer _____

12. basic _____

Read each sentence. Choose a word from above to complete the sentence. Write it on the line.

13. A _____ gave us directions to the park.

14. A band was playing _____ .

15. First we took a _____ ride.

16. Then we bought _____ ice cream.

17. We sat by a _____ bush to rest.

18. There we saw a _____ spinning a web.

19. When I got home, I lay down on the _____ .

20. It was so warm and _____ that I fell asleep.

Help your child write new sentences using the words in numbers 1–12.

Name_____

Study the rule. Read each word and circle the vowel that is sounded by itself. Then write each word, dividing it into syllables.

1. magazine _____

2. open _____

3. uniform _____

4. disagree _____

5. ahead _____

6. Canada _____

7. unit· _____

8. telephone _____

9. disobey _____

10. alive _____

11. ocean _____

12. electric _____

13. against _____

14. document _____

15. gasoline _____

16. Mexico _____

17. eternal _____

18. monument _____

19. odor _____

20. ago _____

Write a paragraph about a place you would like to visit, using as many of the words in numbers 1–20 as you can.

_____

_____

_____

_____

_____

_____

Read each sentence. Choose a word from the box to complete the sentence. Write it on the line.

1. Tory's family went to _____ .

2. Every day they swam in the _____ .

3. The marketplace was _____ .

4. Many _____ were for sale.

5. Tory brought a _____ to read.

6. The family climbed a huge _____ .

7. It had been built a long time _____ .

8. A man in a _____
   explained its history.

9. Tory ran down the steps _____ of her parents.

10. Then she wanted to run up the steps _____ !

pyramid
magazine
uniform
items
ahead
ocean
again
ago
open
Mexico

Write the words from the box above, dividing them into syllables.

11. _____   16. _____

12. _____   17. _____

13. _____   18. _____

14. _____   19. _____

15. _____   20. _____

   Using the words in the box, help your child to make up a new story.

Name _____

▶ **Study the rule. Then write each word, dividing it into syllables.**

1. giant _____
2. quiet _____
3. rodeo _____
4. radiator _____
5. graduate _____
6. dial _____
7. usual _____
8. science _____
9. poem _____
10. radio _____

11. lion _____
12. diet _____
13. ruin _____
14. cruel _____
15. pioneer _____
16. poet _____
17. create _____
18. idea _____
19. gradual _____
20. oriole _____

▶ **Write two sentences using some of the words in numbers 1–20.**

_____
_____
_____
_____
_____

Write each word, dividing it into syllables.

1. radio _____

2. piano _____

3. diet _____

4. diaper _____

5. quiet _____

6. cruel _____

7. graduate _____

8. poem _____

9. lion _____

10. violin _____

11. violet _____

12. giant _____

13. guardian _____

14. create _____

15. rodeo _____

16. dandelion _____

17. Ohio _____

18. science _____

19. idea _____

20. denial _____

21. radiator _____

22. fluid _____

23. ruin _____

24. trial _____

25. theater _____

26. pioneer _____

27. hyena _____

28. celebrate _____

29. realize _____

30. annual _____

31. dial _____

32. violent _____

**Syllables: Words with two vowels together
that are sounded separately**

Ask your child questions that can
be answered with words on the
page, such as *What does a baby
wear? (diaper)*

Name _____

Study the rule. Then write each word, dividing it into syllables.

> When a word ends in **le** preceded by a consonant, divide the word before that consonant.
>
> **nim-ble**

1. turtle _____
2. puzzle _____
3. gentle _____
4. whistle _____
5. eagle _____
6. maple _____
7. pebble _____
8. simple _____
9. thistle _____
10. circle _____
11. purple _____
12. bicycle _____

13. needle _____
14. riddle _____
15. people _____
16. rattle _____
17. scramble _____
18. cradle _____
19. dimple _____
20. sample _____
21. thimble _____
22. temple _____
23. tattle _____
24. middle _____

Write a short paragraph using some of the words in numbers 1–24.

_____

_____

_____

_____

Read the story. Circle each word that contains le preceded by a consonant. Then write each circled word below, dividing it into syllables.

A Day at the Lake

One day, Mary and her dad rode their bicycles to a small lake. They parked the bikes under a maple tree and headed for the boat dock. A gentle breeze made the water ripple.

"I'll show you how to handle a canoe," said Dad. "It's simple. You'll be able to do it in no time."

The man at the dock untied a dark purple canoe and held it against the dock. Mary and her dad stepped squarely into the middle of the canoe so it wouldn't topple.

Mary's dad showed her how to use the paddle as a rudder at the end of each stroke to keep the canoe from going in a circle. Then Mary tried it.

"You're very nimble," said Dad. "You must have strong muscles. You are really doing well."

Mary was proud. She had learned to manage a canoe without any trouble.

1. _____   2. _____   3. _____

4. _____   5. _____   6. _____

7. _____   8. _____   9. _____

10. _____   11. _____   12. _____

13. _____   14. _____   15. _____

 Will Mary and her dad go canoeing again? Why or why not?

 Help your child to continue the story using words from the page.

Name_____

Phonics & Spelling

Say and spell each word. Write the word under the heading where it belongs.

bicycle	magic	purple
comfortable	middle	rebuilding
defrost	misbehaves	science
discovered	open	unkindly
frozen	pioneer	wagon

Words With Prefixes, Suffixes, or Endings

_____

_____

_____

_____

_____

Words With Final le

_____

_____

_____

Two Vowels Together Sounded Separately

_____

_____

One Consonant Between Two Vowels

_____

_____

_____

 Phonics & Writing

A **letter to the editor** is a letter you write to a newspaper. In the letter, you let other people know how you feel about something.

Write a letter to the editor of your local newspaper. Tell why people in your city or town should take good care of the earth. Some of the words in the box may help you.

unkindly	bicycle	outdoors	open	comfortable
planet	rebuilding	discovered	middle	science

Write **today's date** at the top of your letter.

Begin the letter with "Dear Editor," making sure to include a comma.

Tell what you want people to know in the body of the letter.

Sincerely, ...

End your letter with a **closing** and your **name**.

Review prefixes, base words, suffixes and endings, syllables: Writing

 HOME

Point to words in the letter your child wrote. Ask him or her to divide the words into syllables.

Name _____

David's Wonderful Idea

David was discouraged as he slowly rode his bicycle home from school. Everywhere he looked there was litter. There were candy wrappers on lawns and empty milk cartons by the roadside. He even discovered newspapers that had blown up against the trash cans on the sidewalk. The litter was spoiling the outdoors.

1

FOLD

By the end of the day, every piece of litter had disappeared. Newspapers waiting to be recycled were stacked next to neatly tied trashbags.

Someone called, "Three cheers for David. This was all his idea!"

"Hip, hip, hooray!" the crowd exclaimed. David's face wore the biggest smile ever.

4

Suddenly, David had an idea. "Maybe we can have a litter drive. I could talk to my friends and neighbors," he thought.

At dinner that night, David told his parents about his plan. "That sounds like a wonderful idea," Mom said.

Dad said, "Your mother and I will help. I bet a lot of people will be interested in your plan."

2

David talked to his friends about the litter drive. His parents visited neighbors to share the idea. David also put up giant posters to advertise the date of the litter drive.

When the day arrived, many people from the neighborhood came. Those who were unable to come had given rakes, brooms, and trash bags. Soon everyone was working to make the neighborhood clean again!

3

Read each clue. Fill in the circle next to the prefix or suffix that will make a new word that matches the clue. Write the new word on the line.

1. use <u>again</u>   _____   ○ re-   ○ -ful   ○ mis-

2. not <u>usual</u>   _____   ○ -ly   ○ un-   ○ re-

3. <u>behaves</u> badly   _____   ○ mis-   ○ un-   ○ de-

4. giving <u>help</u>   _____   ○ -ful   ○ -ly   ○ ex-

5. not <u>pleased</u>   _____   ○ re-   ○ ex-   ○ dis-

6. to take away the <u>frost</u> _____   ○ un-   ○ de-   ○ -ly

Read each word. Then fill in the circle beside the word that shows how to divide the word into syllables.

7. earth   ○ ear-th   ○ earth   ○ e-arth

8. sunset   ○ suns-et   ○ sunset   ○ sun-set

9. replanted   ○ re-plant-ed   ○ rep-lant-ed   ○ replant-ed

10. better   ○ be-tter   ○ bett-er   ○ bet-ter

11. robin   ○ rob-in   ○ ro-bin   ○ ro-bi-n

12. magic   ○ mag-ic   ○ ma-gic   ○ magi-c

13. quiet   ○ qu-i-et   ○ quie-t   ○ qui-et

14. monument   ○ mo-nu-ment   ○ mon-u-ment   ○ monu-ment

15. purple   ○ pu-rple   ○ purp-le   ○ pur-ple

16. music   ○ mus-ic   ○ mu-sic   ○ m-u-sic

 Read each sentence. Circle the word or words with a prefix, suffix, or ending.

1. News about Earth may discourage you.

2. We cannot always rebuild what we harm.

3. We cannot turn dirty water into clean water overnight.

4. We know that the future of many kinds of animals is uncertain.

5. Many people treat Earth and animals improperly.

6. However, many more people are thoughtful.

7. Many people work hard for a comfortable, safe planet.

8. Earth can renew itself.

9. We must be hopeful about the future.

10. You can make a difference by pitching in to do your part!

Write the base word of each word you circled.

11. _____   16. _____

12. _____   17. _____

13. _____   18. _____

14. _____   19. _____

15. _____   20. _____

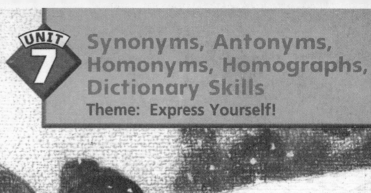

Changing

by Mary Ann Hoberman

I know what I feel like;
I'd like to be *you*
And feel what *you* feel like
And do what *you* do.

I'd like to change places
For maybe a week
And look like your look-alike
And speak as you speak
And think what you're thinking
And go where you go
And feel what you're feeling
And know what you know.

I wish we could do it;
What fun it would be
If I could try you out
And you could try me.

What things about you make you special?

Dear Family,

In this unit, called "Express Yourself," your child will learn about **synonyms** such as **big** and **large**; **antonyms** such as **lost** and **found**; **homonyms** such as **blue/blew**, and **homographs** such as **play**, which has several meanings. Your child will also be learning dictionary skills. As your child explores these skills, you might like to try these activities together.

▶ Have your child write a list of words that describe himself or herself. Then help your child write a second list of words that are synonyms and draw a picture to go with the words.

▶ With your child, read the poem on page 185. Ask your child to identify words with synonyms, antonyms, homonyms, and homographs.

▶ Your child might enjoy reading these books with you. Look for them in your local library.

How to Be Cool in the Third Grade by Betsy Duffey

Louise Goes Wild by Stephen Krensky

Sincerely,

Estimada familia:

En esta unidad, que trata sobre "Express Yourself" ("Expresándote"), su hijo/a estudiará **sinónimos** como **big** (grande) y **large** (amplio); **antónimos** como **lost** (perdido) y **found** (encontrado); **homónimos** como **blue** (azul)**/blew** (sopló) y **homógrafos** como **play** (jugar), que tienen varios significados. También aprenderá a usar un diccionario. A medida que su hijo/a se vaya familiarizando con estas destrezas, pueden hacer las siguientes actividades juntos.

▶ Pidan a su hijo/a que escriba una lista de palabras que lo/a describen. Ayuden a su hijo/a a escribir una segunda lista de palabras que son sinónimos. Pídanle que haga un dibujo de sí mismo/a para acompañar las palabras.

▶ Lean juntos el poema en la página 185. Pidan a su hijo/a que identifique las palabras con sinónimos, antónimos, homónimos, y homógrafos.

▶ Ustedes y su hijo/a disfrutarán leyendo estos libros juntos. Búsquenlos en su biblioteca local.

How to Be Cool in the Third Grade de Betsy Duffey

Louise Goes Wild de Stephen Krensky

Sinceramente,

Name_____

Read each sentence. Then rewrite it, replacing the underlined word with a synonym from the box.

closes	discovers	field	forgets	glad
happens	loud	pretty	radio	silent
tale	teaches	unhappy	upset	woods

1. My dad enjoys reading me a <u>story</u> before bedtime. _____

_____

2. I am <u>happy</u> when we spend time together. _____

_____

3. He begins to read when I am <u>quiet</u>. _____

_____

4. He always <u>finds</u> a new story to read. _____

_____

5. This story is about a girl who lives in the <u>forest</u>. _____

_____

6. She wears a <u>beautiful</u> red cape. _____

_____

7. I can't wait to find out what <u>occurs</u>. _____

_____

What story do you think the girl's dad read to her? How can you tell?

Read each riddle. Write a word from the box to answer the riddle.

big	beautiful	boat	close	funny	hear	woods

1. I have four letters. I mean the same as <u>listen</u>. I am _____.

2. I have five letters. I mean the same as <u>comical</u>. I am _____.

3. I have four letters. I mean the same as <u>ship</u>. I am _____.

4. I have five letters. I mean the same as <u>near</u>. I am _____.

5. I have three letters. I mean the same as <u>large</u>. I am _____.

6. I have five letters. I mean the same as <u>forest</u>. I am _____.

7. I have nine letters. I mean the same as <u>pretty</u>. I am _____.

For each group of words, draw a line from the word in the first column to its synonym in the second column.

8.		9.		10.	
fix	hurt	huge	said	say	drop
injure	gift	pretty	large	fall	little
present	repair	told	quiet	glisten	hard
raise	remain	silent	glad	difficult	tell
stay	lift	happy	beautiful	small	sparkle

11.		12.		13.	
fearful	crawl	street	road	powerful	trip
rare	sad	fast	unhappy	strike	piece
creep	afraid	sad	hurry	journey	strong
big	unusual	rush	closes	store	hit
unhappy	large	shuts	quick	part	shop

HOME

Have your child use some of the words on the page to make up synonym riddles for you to answer, similar to those in numbers 1–7.

Name _____

 For each group of words, draw a line from the word in the first column to its antonym in the second column.

1.
strong	dark
hot	cold
many	few
light	weak

2.
light	tight
loose	warm
cool	heavy
fat	thin

3.
large	fearful
sharp	dull
sick	healthy
fearless	small

4.
asleep	fast
slow	awake
friend	enemy
full	empty

5.
swiftly	quiet
noisy	slowly
difficult	go
come	easy

6.
hard	under
young	soft
above	old
over	below

 Read each sentence. Circle the word that makes each sentence tell about the picture. Write the new sentence on the line.

7. Danny and Fran (climbed, descended) a hill.

_____

8. It was (easy, difficult) to go up the steep hill.

_____

9. Along the path, they saw many (dull, sharp) rocks.

_____

10. When they reached the top, they were (happy, sad).

_____

Read each word. Write its antonym in the blanks. Write the letters from the boxes to answer the question.

above	clear	enemy	healthy	loose	outside
over	separate	sharp	simple	tall	wide

1. tight   _ _ ☐ _ _

2. friend   _ _ _ _ _

3. join   _ _ ☐ _ _ _ _

4. difficult   _ _ _ ☐ _ _

5. under   ☐ _ _ _

6. inside   _ _ ☐ _ _ _

7. smoky   _ _ _ _ _

8. narrow   _ ☐ _ _

9. short   ☐ _ _ _

10. sick   _ ☐ _ _ _ _

11. below   _ _ _ _

12. dull   ☐ _ _ _ _

? **What are antonyms?** _____

HOME Help your child to name other antonym pairs and explain their meanings.

Name _____

▶ **Read each sentence. Circle the word that completes the sentence and write it on the line.**

1. My soccer team (beat, beet) every team this year.   _____

2. We (maid, made) it to the city finals.   _____

3. We (road, rode) to the big game in a bus.   _____

4. We wore our new (blew, blue) uniforms.   _____

5. "Play (fair, fare)," said our coach.   _____

6. Then he (sent, cent) us out onto the field.   _____

7. The time went (buy, by) fast.   _____

8. We (eight, ate) oranges at half time.   _____

9. We couldn't (wait, weight) to continue the game.   _____

10. The game lasted one (our, hour).   _____

11. Katie's goal (won, one) the game for us.   _____

12. The team's picture will (bee, be) in the newspaper.   _____

13. Our trophy will arrive next (weak, week).   _____

 How do you think the team will feel about playing together next year?

Homonyms: Words in context, critical thinking   **191**

Read each sentence. Circle the word that completes the sentence. Write it on the line.

1. _____ have a favorite hobby.   Eye   I

2. I like to _____ with my brother.   sail   sale

3. He _____ many things about boats.   nose   knows

4. He is teaching me to tie a square _____.   knot   not

5. Last week he _____ me practice.   maid   made

6. I still can't tie it the _____ way.   right   write

7. We sail _____ boat every weekend.   hour   our

8. We will sail today _____ tomorrow.   oar   or

9. We must _____ for the wind to blow.   wait   weight

For each group of words, draw a line from the word in the first column to its homonym in the second column.

10.

break   knot
not   stake
weight   wait
steak   brake

11.

ate   wrap
ring   wring
rap   eight
bare   bear

12.

right   dye
see   sea
die   road
rode   write

13.

I   pane
led   sale
sail   eye
pain   lead

Help your child to name other homonym pairs and explain the meaning of each word.

Name _____

Read the passage. Then write a homonym from the passage to complete each sentence.

Art From the Paper World

George Pocheptsov, or "Georgie" as he is called, started to paint before he was two years old. He sold his first painting by the age of three. By the time he was eight, Georgie's art was selling for thousands of dollars apiece! Many people want to buy his paintings because they are so bright and colorful.

Georgie's favorite things to paint include animals, sea creatures, and people with musical instruments. He draws every day, sometimes for hours at a time. First he uses a pencil to make just the right sketch. Then he fills in the sketch with paints.

Before Georgie begins to paint, he visits his "paper world." This world is in his head. That's where all his ideas come from. Georgie says, "I want people to look at my paintings and see that the world is beautiful."

1. Georgie started to paint before he was _____ .

2. By the time he was _____, his art was selling for thousands of dollars.

3. Many people want to _____ Georgie's paintings.

4. Georgie sometimes draws for _____ at a time.

5. Georgie uses a pencil to make just the _____ sketch.

6. Georgie wants people to _____ that the world is beautiful.

 What are your favorite things to draw or paint? Why are they your favorites?

A **narrative paragraph** tells a story about something that really happened. The events, characters, and setting are real. Often the writer is the main character.

> **Write a narrative paragraph to tell people about something interesting that you did or that happened to you. Some of the words in the box may help you.**

I	right	eight	eye	wear
where	hour	ate	write	our

Begin with a **topic sentence** that tells who, when, and where.

_____

_____

_____

Use words like *first*, *then*, and *later* to make the **order** of the story clear.

_____

_____

_____

_____

_____

Use words that tell how things **looked**, **sounded**, **smelled**, **tasted**, and **felt**.

_____

_____

_____

Help your child to think of sentences that use homonyms, such as *The wind blew the blue boat.*

Name_____

► **Read the hint. Then write each list of words in alphabetical order.**

1.

foxes _____

goat _____

beaver _____

camel _____

deer _____

antelope _____

elephant _____

2.

Danny _____

Ann _____

Frank _____

Carl _____

Betty _____

Ellen _____

Gerry _____

3.

bicycle _____

bat _____

bubbles _____

blocks _____

boat _____

break _____

4.

cheese _____

chop _____

chrome _____

chair _____

children _____

chuckle _____

Look at each pair of guide words and the words below them. Circle the words in each list that you would find on a page with those guide words.

Guide words appear at the top of each dictionary page. They tell you what the first and last words on the page are. All the words on the page are in alphabetical order between the guide words.

1.
mice • mop
mile
men
mitt
moon
mask

2.
fish • gate
five
frogs
girl
gave
fun

3.
dance • day
dark
deer
doll
date
dawn

4.
rabbit • rake
radio
raccoon
rocket
radish
rain

5.
wagon • wax
wallet
wooden
watching
watermelon
whale

6.
present • print
pretzel
princess
propeller
principal
press

HOME Help your child to think of other words that could be found between the guide words on this page.

Name _____

> Look at each pair of guide words. Write the word from the box that belongs between the guide words.

candle	drapes	jar	race	sandwiches	window
deal	flowers	lantern	rectangle	thirteen	zero

1. sailboat   _____ saw

2. dragon   _____ dressing

3. flat   _____ flute

4. jacket   _____ jay

5. ladder   _____ lazy

6. record   _____ red

7. think   _____ thorn

8. camel   _____ candy

9. whiskers   _____ wishbone

10. dazzle   _____ dear

11. zebra   _____ zigzag

12. rabbit   _____ raffle

> Look at each pair of guide words and the dictionary page number. Write the page number on which you would find each word listed below.

each • elevator 210	**elf • escape** 215	**fake • frown** 243

13. elephant _____   14. favorite _____   15. erase _____

16. easel _____   17. English _____   18. farmer _____

19. family _____   20. educate _____   21. eggplant _____

> Read each pair of guide words. Circle the five words in the box that would appear between those guide words. Then write the words you circled in alphabetical order on the lines.

1.

(can • cave)

candy	_____
case	_____
cold	_____
carve	_____
carton	_____
cap	

2.

(hide • hit)

hen	_____
hire	_____
hilly	_____
hiker	_____
hip	_____
himself	

3.

(sad • saw)

same	_____
soap	_____
save	_____
sand	_____
sail	_____
salad	

4.

(train • truck)

treetop	_____
trap	_____
trot	_____
travel	_____
tail	_____
tray	

Ask your child to explain how he or she would alphabetize these words: *raincoat, rainy, rainbow, raindrop.*

198   Dictionary: Guide words

Name_____

Where in the dictionary would you find the words in the box? Write each word where it belongs.

> **HINT**
> Dictionary words are listed in alphabetical order. You can find a word quickly if you think of the dictionary as having three parts: **Beginning Letters** (A–I), **Middle Letters** (J–Q), and **Ending Letters** (R–Z).

aunt	sister	doctor	myself	father
joy	love	teacher	family	write
read	brother	mother	uncle	neighbor

Beginning (A–I)	**Middle (J–Q)**	**End (R–Z)**
1. _____	2. _____	3. _____
4. _____	5. _____	6. _____
7. _____	8. _____	9. _____
10. _____	11. _____	12. _____
13. _____	14. _____	15. _____

Write Beginning, Middle, or End to tell where in the dictionary each word in bold print can be found.

16. People **express** themselves in different ways. _____

17. Some people **write** books or poetry. _____

18. Athletes **play** many different sports. _____

19. Dancers such as Rosa express themselves with

    their **bodies**. _____

20. How do you express **yourself**? _____

Read the information in each exercise. Then answer the questions. Use page 199 to help you.

1.

You are writing a science report on dinosaurs. Look up the word *Tyrannosaurus.* In which section of the dictionary would you find this word? _____

You open the dictionary and see the guide words **unbroken • undergo**. Would *Tyrannosaurus* come **before, on,** or **after** a page with those guide words? _____

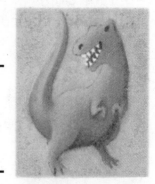

2.

While reading a recipe, you see the word *barbecue.* Where in the dictionary will you find this word? _____

You open the dictionary and see the guide words **by • category**. Would *barbecue* come **before, on,** or **after** a page with those guide words? _____

3.

In a book of old Roman myths, you see the word *Hercules*. In which section of the dictionary should you look to find this word? _____

You open the dictionary and see the guide words **hen • hero**. Would *Hercules* come **before, on,** or **after** a page with those guide words? _____

4.

You want to know more about North America. Look up *North America*. In which section of the dictionary would you find these words? _____

You open the dictionary and see the guide words **music • nap**. Would *North America* come **before, on,** or **after** a page with those guide words? _____

Ask your child to name favorite activities such as *basketball* or *reading*, then tell you in which section of the dictionary those words would be found.

Name_____

Look at each picture. Read the dictionary entries next to it. In the box, write the number of the entry whose definition goes with the picture.

DEFINITION
Sometimes you will see two or more entry words in a dictionary that have different meanings but are spelled the same way. These words are called **homographs.**

1.

loaf¹   a portion of bread or cake baked in a definite form

loaf²   to idle away time

2.

bat-ter¹   to beat very hard

bat-ter²   a thick mixture of flour, milk, or water, and eggs beaten together for use in cooking

bat-ter³   a person who bats, in baseball or cricket

3.

mole¹   a small spot on the skin, usually dark and slightly raised

mole²   a small, furry animal with poor eyesight that lives underground

4.

scale¹   one of the thin, flat plates that covers the body of certain animals

scale²   a device for weighing

scale³   (in music) a series of tones either going up or going down

Read each pair of dictionary entries and the sentence below them. Choose the entry whose definition fits the meaning of the underlined word. Write the entry number, 1 or 2, in the box.

1.

prune¹ a variety of plum that dries without spoiling

prune² to cut off or trim twigs or branches

Grandpa will <u>prune</u> the bushes in his garden.

2.

fine¹ very good

fine² money paid as a penalty for breaking a law

Meg did a <u>fine</u> job of painting the bookshelves.

3.

spoke¹ the past tense of **speak**

spoke² a bar coming out of the hub of a wheel

Danny had to repair two of the <u>spokes</u> on his bike.

4.

bat¹ a wooden club used to hit a ball, as in baseball or cricket

bat² a flying mammal, active at night

As they entered the cave, a <u>bat</u> flew out.

5.

ring¹ a circular band worn on the finger as an ornament

ring² to give forth a clear sound, as a doorbell or telephone bell

The bride and groom wore matching gold <u>rings</u>.

6.

case¹ a situation or condition, as in *a sad case*

case² a container

Janet put her new pin in her jewelry <u>case</u>.

7.

post¹ an upright piece of timber or metal

post² a position to which a person is assigned

Claude hammered the fence <u>post</u> into the ground.

8.

mail¹ letters or packages that are delivered by the post office

mail² armor made of metal rings linked together

Fran got <u>mail</u> from her pen pal in Australia.

Help your child think of a sentence using the other meaning in each set.

Name _____

Phonics & Spelling

Find the synonym in the box for each word.
Write it on the line.

| display | find | quick | raise |

1. show _____
2. locate _____
3. swift _____
4. lift _____

Find the antonym in the box for each word.
Write it on the line.

| come | high | light | something |

5. nothing _____
6. low _____
7. heavy _____
8. go _____

Write a homonym for each word.

9. right _____
10. buy _____
11. dear _____
12. stare _____

An **e-mail message** is a message you write and send to someone on a computer. Both you and the person you're writing to must have a computer, access to the Internet, and an e-mail address.

Write an e-mail message to a friend. Tell your friend about someplace you would like to go with him or her. Some of the words in the box may help you. Make up an e-mail address for the person you are writing to.

here	come	write	hear	park
stay	right	drive	play	there

Write your friend's e-mail address after the "To."

Write what the message is about after the "Subject."

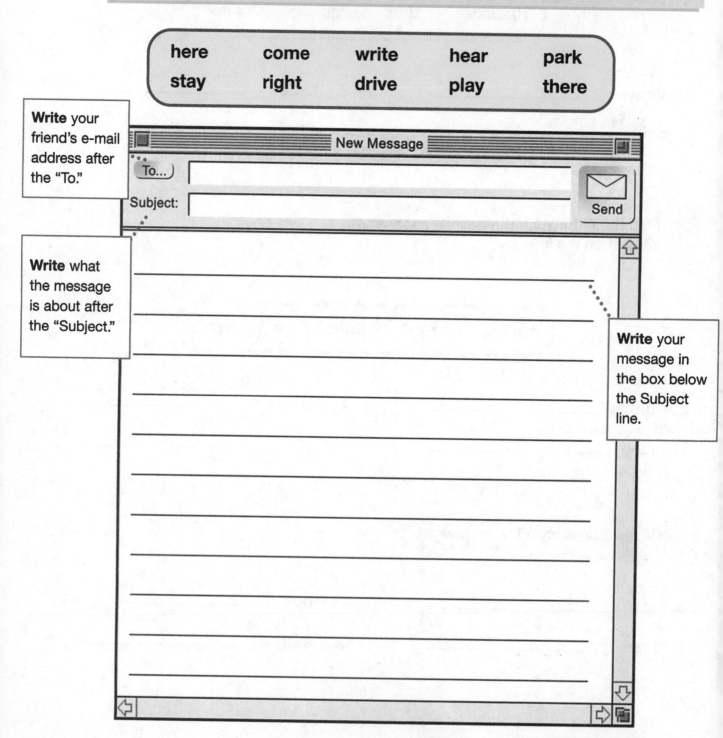

New Message

To...

Subject:

Send

Write your message in the box below the Subject line.

204 Review synonyms, antonyms, homonyms: Writing

HOME

Point to words in the e-mail your child wrote. Ask him or her to identify any synonyms, antonyms, or homonyms for the words.

Name _____

A little Imagination

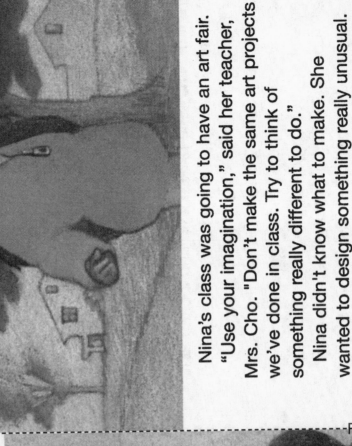

Nina's class was going to have an art fair. "Use your imagination," said her teacher, Mrs. Cho. "Don't make the same art projects we've done in class. Try to think of something really different to do."

Nina didn't know what to make. She wanted to design something really unusual. She thought about the project as she walked home from school.

1

--- FOLD ---

The day of the art fair arrived, and the children set up their projects. As Mrs. Cho walked around the room, she paused in front of each work. She stayed by Nina's picture for a long time.

"You all worked very hard," Mrs. Cho said at last. "It isn't easy to choose just one winner, but I think Nina deserves the blue ribbon. Her picture is certainly different, and it's not just an art project—it's a science lesson, too!"

4

A maple seed fluttered down to the ground in front of Nina. She picked it up and looked at it. With its two wings, it looked a little like a bird. That gave Nina an idea. What if she made a picture from seeds? She could use the maple seed and some apple seeds. She also remembered saving dried pumpkin seeds last fall, though she forgot exactly where they were. She raced the rest of the way home. She could hardly wait to get started.

2

FOLD

Her mother was baking bread. She wiped the flour off her hands and reached in a cupboard. "Here are our pumpkin seeds," Mom said. "I have some new flower seed packets you can use, too."

Nina glued the maple seed to the top of a sheet of paper. It made a beautiful bird. She used pumpkin seeds to make pretty clouds. At the bottom of the picture she formed flowers from different seeds.

3

Name _____

▶ Read each pair of words. Decide whether they are
synonyms, antonyms, or homonyms. Fill in the circle.

	Synonyms	Antonyms	Homonyms
1. right/write	○	○	○
2. right/wrong	○	○	○
3. display/show	○	○	○
4. high/low	○	○	○
5. here/hear	○	○	○

▶ Read the word. Fill in the circle beside the guide words
under which the entry word would be listed.

6. diet	○ dig-dip	○ debt-dent	○ did-different
7. ramp	○ ran-rap	○ rake-rang	○ rabbit-rag
8. custom	○ cost-cup	○ cup-cut	○ come-couple
9. ocean	○ oar-odor	○ ouch-over	○ one-opera
10. limb	○ lick-like	○ list-little	○ lima-lint

▶ Write the words in the box in alphabetical order.

11. _____

12. _____

13. _____

14. _____

15. _____

16. _____

> display
> detract
> decide
> distance
> determine
> demand

Synonyms, antonyms, homonyms, dictionary skills: Assessment **207**

> **Read the sentence. Choose the meaning of the word that is used in the sentence. Write the number of the meaning beside the sentence.**

scale¹   one of the thin, flat plates that cover the body of certain animals

scale²   a device for weighing

scale³   (in music) a series of tones either going up or going down

spoke¹   the past tense of speak

spoke²   a bar coming out of the hub of a wheel

batter¹   a thick mixture of flour, milk, or water, and eggs beaten together for use in cooking

batter²   a person who bats, in baseball or cricket

fine¹   very good

fine²   money paid as a penalty for breaking a law

_____ 1. Amy mixed the **batter** for a surprise birthday cake.

_____ 2. Jason **spoke** to his class about his favorite hobby.

_____ 3. Mrs. Hadley paid a **fine** when her parking meter ran out.

_____ 4. The school nurse weighed pupils on a new **scale**.

> **Circle the word that finishes each sentence.**

5. There is (no, know) person exactly like you.

6. You may like (to, too) play ball or swim.

7. Do you like the color (blew, blue)?

8. What day of the (weak, week) is your favorite?

9. Do you have a favorite poem or (tail, tale)?

10. What kind of music do you like to (here, hear)?

11. Do you like to learn (new, knew) sports?

12. (Wear, Where) is your favorite place to visit?

PEARSON
Phonics
LEVEL C Elwell • Murray • Kucia

ILLUSTRATIONS: Page 140: Elizabeth Allen. 110: Meryl Anderson. 45: Bob Berry. 154: Gary Bialke. 105,145 Lisa Blackshear. 3, 137, 139: Denny Bond. 196: Greta Buchart. 67, 102, 172, 192: Annette Cable. 81: Penny Carter. 47: Cat Graphics. 166: Michael Chesworth. 129: Chi Chung. 108, 195: Daniel Clifford. 185: Raul Colon. 40: Nancy Doniger. 93: Julie Durrell. 58: Allan Eitzen. 115, 135 178: Doris Ettlinger. 1, 114: Peter Fasolino. 23: Siri Weber Feeney. 96, 138: Julia Gorton. 19, 20: Laurie Harden. 4, 111, 169, 170, 197: Dennis Hockerman. 70: Jeff Hopkins. 205, 206: Laura Jacobsen. 4, 14, 122, 131, 163, 181, 182: Meredith Johnson. 80: John Kanzler. 200: Wallace Keller. 113: Anne Kennedy. 29, 101, 171: Terry Kovalcik. 2, 72: Holly Kowitt. 66: Darcia Labrosse. 153: Jeff Le Van. 136, 160: Anthony Lewis. 53: Lori Lohstoeter. 8, 56, 107: Diana Magnuson. 73: Shelley Matheis. 94, 168: Anni Matsick. 32, 62: Erin Mauterer. 157: Patrick Merrell. 1, 15, 16: Andy Myer. 95: Mary Newell. 6, 130: Pearson Learning. 30: Donna Perrone. 77: Mick Reid. 26, 38, 133: Janet Skiles. 12: Michael Sloan. 85: Teri Sloat. 10: Valerie Sokolova. 158: Jessica Wolk-Stanley. 76: Tom Stanley. 13: Sara Swan. 41: Winson Trang. 191: Amy Wummer. 55,189: Amy Young.116: Jerry Zimmerman.

ACKNOWLEDGMENTS: "Changing" from *The Llama Who Had No Pajama: 100 Favorite Poems*, copyright © 1981 by Mary Ann Hoberman, reprinted by permission of Harcourt, Inc. Reprinted by permission of Gina Maccoby Literary Agency in the British Commonwealth. Copyright © 1959, renewed 1987, 1998 by Mary Ann Hoberman. "The Spangled Pandemonium" from *Beyond The Paw Paw Trees* by Palmer Brown. Copyright © 1954 by Palmer Brown. Used by permission of HarperCollins Publishers. Edite Kroll Literary Agency for the British Commonwealth. Excerpt from the poem "Reply to Someone Who Asked…" in *A Week In The Life Of Best Friends* by Beatrice Schenk de Regniers. Copyright © 1986 by Beatrice Schenk de Regniers. Used by permission of Marian Reiner.

NOTE: Every effort has been made to locate the copyright owner of material reprinted in this book. Omissions brought to our attention will be corrected in subsequent printings.

PHOTOGRAPHS: Cover: © Henk Bentlage/Shutterstock. Page 5: © Satin/Fotolia. 6: *m.* © Getty Images/Hemera Technologies/Thinkstock. 7: *tr.* © Roger Scott/Fotolia, *mtl.* © Getty Images/Thinkstock, *mtmr.* © Tony Campbell/Fotolia, *mbl.* © Victoria Liu/Fotolia, *mbmr.* © StarJumper/Fotolia, *mtml.* © Simone van den Berg/Fotolia, *tl.* © Getty Images/Hemera Technologies/Thinkstock, *tml.* © Jupiterimages/Thinkstock, *tmr.* © Brand X Pictures/Thinkstock, *mtr.* © Lasse Kristensen/Fotolia, *mbml.* © Getty Images/Hemera Technologies/Thinkstock, *mbr.* © Zee/Fotolia, *bl.* © paul prescott/Fotolia, *bml.* © Iryna Volina/Fotolia, *bmr.* © Brand X Pictures/Thinkstock, *br.* © Studio Gi/Fotolia. 9: *mbl.* © Konstantin Kikvidze/Fotolia, *mbml.* © Vladimir Melnik/Fotolia, *bl.* © Bayou Jeff/Fotolia, *bml.* © Johnaalex/Fotolia, *tl.* © VanHart/Fotolia, *tml.* © Getty Images/Hemera Technologies/Thinkstock, *tmr.* © Tommy/Fotolia, *tr.* © Stockbyte/Thinkstock, *mtl.* © Auremar/Fotolia, *mtml.* © Les Cunliffe/Fotolia, *mtmr.* © Thomas Northcut/Thinkstock, *mtr.* © Zedcor Wholly Owned/Thinkstock, *mbmr.* © nedjenn/Fotolia, *bmr.* © Akiyoko/Fotolia, *br.* © Joss/Fotolia, *mbr.* © Iznogood/Fotolia. 24: *m.* © Shock/Fotolia. 27: *tml.* © DC Productions/Thinkstock, *tmr.* © Hemera Technologies/Thinkstock, *tr.* © Victoria Liu/Fotolia, *bl.* © Vivalapenler/Fotolia, *l.* © Ablestock.com/Thinkstock, *bmr.* © Comstock/Thinkstock, *br.* © Bert Folsom/Fotolia, *tl.* © Iznogood/Fotolia. 28: *r.* © Victoria Liu/Fotolia, *l.* © Vasiliy Koval/Fotolia. 29: *bl.* © Lisa Turay/Fotolia, *bml.* © Yxowert/Fotolia, *br.* © Abderit99/Fotolia, *tl.* © r-o-x-o-r/Fotolia, *tml.* © Getty Images/Hemera Technologies/Thinkstock, *tmr.* © Getty Images/Hemera Technologies/Thinkstock, *bmr.* © Michael Kempf/Fotolia, *tr.* © Elaine Barker/Fotolia. 31: *bl.* © Jupiterimages/Thinkstock, *tl.* © Stockbyte/Thinkstock, *tml.* © Picture Partners/Fotolia, *tmr.* © Graça Victoria/Fotolia, *tr.* © Sotern/Fotolia, *bml.* © Borys Shevchuk/Fotolia, *bmr.* © Imate/Fotolia, *br.* © Olga Sapegina/Fotolia. 33: *tr.* © Lilyana Vynogradova/Fotolia, *mml.* © Hemera Technologies/Thinkstock, *mr.* © Gravicapa/Fotolia, *tl.* © Thinkstock, *tml.* © Svyatoslav Lypynskyy/Fotolia, *tmr.* © Hemera Technologies/Thinkstock, *mmr.* © Sneekerp/Fotolia, *bm.* © Sneekerp/Fotolia, *ml.* © Thinkstock, *bl.* © Iznogood/Fotolia. 35: *tr.* © Ipope/Fotolia. 36: *tr.* © Iofoto/Fotolia. 37: *mtm.* © Linous/Fotolia, *bl.* © Jupiterimages/Thinkstock, *tl.* © Ia_64/Fotolia, *tm.* © Brand X Pictures/Thinkstock, *tr.* © Aidaricci/Fotolia, *mtl.* © cretolamna/Fotolia, *mtr.* © Andrzej Tokarski/Fotolia, *mbl.* © Getty Images/Hemera Technologies/Thinkstock, *mbr.* © Jupiterimages/Thinkstock, *bm.* © Close Encounters/Fotolia, *br.* © Kelpfish/Fotolia, *mbm.* © ioannis kounadeas/Fotolia. 39: *mtr.* © Yui/Fotolia, *mbl.* © BananaStock/Thinkstock, *bm.* © Kokhanchikov/Fotolia, *tl.* © James Steidl/Fotolia, *tm.* © M.Camerin/Fotolia, *tr.* © PhotoGraphie/Fotolia, *mtl.* © Igor/Fotolia, *mtm.* © Liron/Fotolia, *mbm.* © Loongir/Fotolia, *mbr.* © Aleksandr Ugorenkov/Fotolia, *bl.* © Getty Images/PhotoObjects.net/Thinkstock, *br.* © Yahia Loukkal/Fotolia. 42: *l.* © Andrzej Tokarski/Fotolia, *m.* © Anetta/Fotolia, *r.* © Milosluz/Fotolia. 43: *tm.* © Thomas Northcut/Thinkstock, *mbl.* © Alexford/Fotolia, *bl.* © Wild Geese/Fotolia, *br.* © Jupiterimages/Thinkstock, *tl.* © Getty Images/Hemera Technologies/Thinkstock, *tr.* © Stockbyte/Thinkstock, *mtl.* © Sparkia/Fotolia, *mtm.* © Gordan Gledec/Fotolia, *mtr.* © Comstock/Thinkstock, *mbm.* © Lev Olkha/Fotolia, *mbl.* © Maksim Shebeko/Fotolia, *bm.* © Alexandra Karamyshev/Fotolia. 49: *t.* © Sheri/Fotolia, *b.* © Hemera Technologies/Thinkstock. 50: *tr.* © Jupiterimages/Thinkstock, *tl.* © Morpheus/Fotolia, *b.* © Dabj/Fotolia. 51: *bl.* © Yxowert/Fotolia, *tl.* © Anetta/Fotolia, *tmr.* © Mario Beauregard/Fotolia, *tr.* © Brand X Pictures/Thinkstock, *bml.* © Stockbyte/Thinkstock, *bmr.* © Sneekerp/Fotolia, *br.* © Solodovnikova Elena/Fotolia, *tml.* © Iznogood/Fotolia. 57: *mbl.* © Jupiterimages/Thinkstock, *mbml.* © Laurent Renault/Fotolia, *bml.* © Victoria Liu/Fotolia, *tl.* © Comstock/Thinkstock, *tml.* © nedjenn/Fotolia, *tmr.* © Hemera Technologies/Thinkstock, *mtl.* © Cphoto/Fotolia, *mtml.* © Gordan Gledec/Fotolia, *mtmr.* © Jupiterimages/Thinkstock, *mtr.* © blue eye/Fotolia, *mbmr.* © Getty Images/Comstock Images/Thinkstock, *mbr.* © Tifonimages/Fotolia, *bl.* © Tommy/Fotolia, *bmr.* © MAXFX/Fotolia, *br.* © Andres Rodriguez/Fotolia, *tr.* © Iznogood/Fotolia. 59: *tm.* © Esweet/Fotolia, *br.* © Jupiterimages/Thinkstock, *tl.* © Hemera Technologies/Getty Images/Thinkstock, *tr.* © Michael Flippo/Fotolia, *bl.* © George Dolgikh/Fotolia, *bm.* © Marc Dietrich/Fotolia. 60: *tl.* © Harris Shiffman/Fotolia, *mtr.* © Esweet/Fotolia, *mbl.* © Jupiterimages/Thinkstock, *mbr.* © Dick Luria/Thinkstock, *bl.* © Wong Hock Weng/Fotolia, *tr.* © Tatty/Fotolia, *mtl.* © Hemera Technologies/Getty Images/Thinkstock, *ml.* © Volff/Fotolia, *mr.* © Hemera Technologies/Getty Images/Thinkstock, *br.* © Michael Flippo/Fotolia. 61: *m.* © Le Do/Fotolia, *mbr.* © Route66Photography/Fotolia, *tl.* © Ivan Stanic/Fotolia, *tm.* © Getty Images/Hemera Technologies/Thinkstock, *tr.* © blue eye/Fotolia, *mtl.* © Edyta Pawlowska/Fotolia, *mtm.* © Berean/Fotolia, *mtr.* © Getty Images/Comstock Images/Thinkstock, *mml.* © Homydesign/Fotolia, *mmr.* © Nymph/Fotolia, *mbl.* © Auremar/Fotolia, *mbm.* © Tifonimages/Fotolia, *bl.* © Getty Images/Thinkstock, *bm.* © Jeka84/Fotolia, *br.* © Yi Liu/Fotolia. 63: *tm.* © Eric Isselée/Fotolia, *m.* © Hemera Technologies/Thinkstock, *mmr.* © Bayou Jeff/Fotolia, *mbl.* © MTC Media/Fotolia, *bl.* © Yahia Loukkal/Fotolia, *bm.* © O.M/Fotolia, *br.* © Jim Mills/Fotolia, *tl.* © Ellypoo/Fotolia, *tr.* © Ryan McVay/Thinkstock, *mtl.* © Ivan Gulei/Fotolia, *mtm.* © Jaimie Duplass/Fotolia, *mtr.* © Getty Images/Comstock Images/Thinkstock, *mml.* © Hemera Technologies/Getty Images/Thinkstock, *mbr.* © Hemera Technologies/Thinkstock, *mbm.* © Atropat/Fotolia. 65: *tmr.* © Duncan Noakes/Fotolia, *tl.* © Hemera Technologies/Getty Images/Thinkstock, *tml.* © Ana Vasileva/Fotolia, *tr.* © George Doyle/Thinkstock, *mtl.* © Elnur/Fotolia, *mtml.* © Stockbyte/Thinkstock, *mtmr.* © Thomas Northcut/Thinkstock, *mtr.* © Jupiterimages/Thinkstock, *mbl.* © StarJumper/Fotolia, *mbml.* © Comstock/Thinkstock, *mbmr.* © Jiri Hera/Fotolia, *mbr.* © Wildman/Fotolia, *bl.* © PhotoObjects.net/Thinkstock, *bml.* © Melking/Fotolia, *bmr.* © Ablestock.com/Thinkstock, *br.* © Hemera Technologies/Getty Images/Thinkstock. 69: *tl.* © Agphotographer/Fotolia, *tml.* © Paul Murphy/Fotolia, *tr.* © Le Do/Fotolia, *bl.* © David De Lossy/Thinkstock, *bml.* © Otmar Smit/Fotolia, *tmr.* © Dleonis/Fotolia, *bmr.* © Stockbyte/Thinkstock, *br.* © Yury Shirokov/Fotolia. 71: *tr.* © Abderit99/Fotolia, *tl.* © Ivaylo Ivanov/Fotolia, *tml.* © Brand X Pictures/Thinkstock, *tmr.* © Bhofack2/Fotolia, *bl.* © Getty Images/Hemera Technologies/Thinkstock, *bml.* © Marsel/Fotolia, *bmr.* © Irochka/Fotolia, *br.* © Dennis Tokarzewski/Fotolia. 74: *tr.* © Kasia Biel/Fotolia. 75: *tml.* © Philippe Leridon/Fotolia, *tr.* © Bayou Jeff/Fotolia, *mtl.* © Irochka/Fotolia, *mtml.* © Duncan Noakes/Fotolia, *mtmr.* © Victoria Liu/Fotolia, *tl.* © Stockbyte/Thinkstock, *tmr.* © Studio Gi/Fotolia, *mtr.* © Veniamin Kraskov/Fotolia, *mbl.* © Auremar/Fotolia, *mbml.* © Tatty/Fotolia,